ELEMENTS OF
HOME DESIGN

PAINT & PAPER

ELEMENTS OF
HOME DESIGN

PAINT & PAPER

KARIN STROM

BARNES
& NOBLE

NEW YORK

A BARNES & NOBLE BOOK

©1999 by Creative Homeowner®, a division of Federal Marketing Corp.
This edition 2005 by Barnes & Noble Publishing, Inc.

ISBN 0-7607-6045-4

Printed and bound in China by Midas Printing International Ltd.

3 5 7 9 10 8 6 4 2

Photography by George Ross except
pages 14–19 and 21 (Christies, New York);
page 20 (the Shelburne Museum)

Acknowledgments

The production of any book is somewhat of a team effort, so there are many people to thank for their presence on the team. First, I want to thank my friend and colleague, Ginger Hansen Shafer, without whom this book wouldn't have been possible. Her talent, taste level, tireless patience, and ability to read my mind are a source of amazement to me. We developed the project designs together, and Ginger exquisitely executed all of them as well as demonstrated all of the how-tos. Thanks also to Mark and Nels for loaning her to me for so long.

Thank you to Kathie Robitz for her calm support of this project and for keeping me laughing throughout. And to Jan Greco for her elegant graphic design. Thanks also to Creative Homeowner Press for letting us break new ground with this book.

Special thanks to George Ross for both his unerring eye and sweet personality, and to his cadre of able assistants for providing both help and entertainment.

Thanks to my dear friend, Ellie Joos, for letting us invade her home for photography, yet again, and for her support. For the use of her garden room, thank you to Alison Barnett.

Last but not least, my love and thanks to Gabe and Colin for putting up with the endless projects and photo shoots, and as always, for their support.

Contents

Introduction

dmittedly, there are various methods for applying painted finishes and decorative techniques, ranging from the extremely complex to the overly simple. And often the presentation of these techniques comes as either a highly technical, cumbersome text or in picture form with little how-to advice. Either way, a nonprofessional—especially a beginner—might find the process downright daunting. *Paint & Paper* covers all the bases. It presents you with lots of different style ideas and ways for personalizing your home with one-of-a

kind furnishings and accessories. A range of terrific-looking projects and techniques involve a few easy-to-understand steps and are eminently doable even if you've never tried them before.

In Part I, A Background, *Paint & Paper* gets you started with "A Brief History of Paint & Paper," a chapter that introduces you to a time-honored tradition. For example, most of the finishing techniques popular today were originally developed centuries ago as a means to create the illusion of something more costly—gilding to imitate gold;

marbling to transform inexpensive wood into elegant stone; decoupage to simulate hand painting.

Following that, the chapter called "Preparation & Tools" will familiarize you with the kinds of paints, brushes, and other materials and implements you'll be using. In "Finishes & Techniques" you'll learn all of the basic steps for each of the methods. Throughout, every effort has been made to simplify each technique as much as possible so as not to scare anyone away. Wherever possible, the projects utilize water-based products, which are both fast-drying and easy to clean up. After carefully reading this chapter, practice your skills before beginning any actual projects. Once you're comfortable with the finishes that interest you, it will become easy to mix and match colors and techniques and develop your own ideas.

In Part II, A House Tour, you'll find projects and decorating tips for every room in your home. Each chapter has been inspired by a theme—a decorating style, a favorite fabric, a color, or a concept. For example, "A French-Country Dining Room" recalls van Gogh's Provence. Its decorating inspiration came from a Provençal-style tablecloth found at a flower show. A lively Noah's Ark wallpaper and coordinating fabric provide a playful motif for "A Child's Room." And fruits and vegetables provide the key ingredients for "A Welcoming Country Kitchen."

Happily, for those who are pressed for time, most of the projects can be completed over a weekend; some in just one afternoon. Naturally, the items that involve several techniques will take a little longer, but the results are well worth the waiting.

You may already have a color scheme or theme for a room and simply want to add some unique touches. Or if you're starting from scratch, go to your favorite fabric store and get a selection of fabric swatches. If the store doesn't cut swatches, buy an eighth of a yard. For beautiful decorative papers, look in museum shops, card shops, and art supply stores. Many paint stores sell wallpaper by the roll. Actual paper works best for decoupage, so stay away from vinyl wallcovering. Purchase a couple of different rolls, and pick up some paint chips. Bring them home, spread them out, and live with them for a while. Something will speak to you. Craft suppliers and many large chain stores carry a fine selection of craft paints, stencils, varnishes, and gilding materials, as well as various-sized brushes.

Some of the items in the book are "reclaimed rejects"—things that are just too good to leave behind. So if you like to frequent junk shops and yard sales, you'll love the idea of recycling and transforming shabby objects into chic ones. When you're on the hunt for treasures, keep your eyes open for classic shapes and interesting detailing, but don't overlook the simplest pieces, which often work best for more-dramatic treatments. A plain pail becomes an instant heirloom when it's covered in a collage of fabulous cutouts. When considering furniture, you can ignore a bad paint job or a loose spindle. But stay away from the chair that has to be entirely reglued or the table that has been sitting out in the rain for an entire summer. Keep an open mind. You may not find exactly what you're looking for,

but there's usually a solution close by. As a rule of thumb, if a piece of furniture is basically sound and the price is right, grab it. If you don't, someone else will. Some of the best bargains in this book include the headboard, which is on page 68 and cost less than $5 in a junk shop, and the chair in the French-country dining room on page 106, which cost just $3. It was a serendipitous flea-market find.

While you may love transforming trash into treasure, it's best to work with unfinished pine pieces in most cases. They're easy to come by, and there's virtually no preparation involved. Because the finish is uniform on the entire piece, the results are more predictable. For certain techniques, such as staining, the virgin surface of unfinished wood makes a better receptor of paint than a recycled one,

even if it has been painstakingly stripped. It's often difficult to get rid of the old finish entirely.

In the "Sources" section, you'll find resources for most of the unfinished pine pieces, papers, fabrics, stencils, stamps, and paints, but feel free to look for others on your own. Starting on page 130, you'll also find additional stencils that you can photocopy and cut out, as well as wallpaper samples, so that you can duplicate or modify any of the design themes in the book.

Whether you choose to redo an entire room or simply add some interesting decorative accents, you're sure to find the inspiration and savoir faire here to get started. Remember, it's the handmade objects, the unusual textures, and the unexpected colors that give a house its unique personality—yours. Enjoy!

PART I:
A BACKGROUND

Decorative finishes have origins that reach far back into time, perhaps much further than you might guess. If you are fascinated by the thought of an ancient Egyptian gilding a chair, imagine a man or a woman painting images on the walls of caves. To give you a sense of the richness of the painted tradition, this section briefly outlines the roots of decorative finishes and their place in history. It also gives you a good start by explaining what you need to gather to prepare yourself for any decorative finishing project, as well as a foundation for applying today's most popular techniques.

While the old ways of decorative painting are admittedly difficult and exacting—and most people don't have the time to learn them nowadays—they have their place. Fortunately, the water-based products and simplified processes in the following chapters will make reproducing them possible for the novice, as well as for the more-experienced decorator.

A Brief History of Paint & Paper

The urge to embellish one's surroundings with painted details seems to have been a natural inclination for human beings that predates civilized societies. Throughout time, from the days when people depicted their daily activities on the walls of their cave dwellings to the fast-paced technological age we live in today, that decorative impulse persists.

Inhabitants of virtually every corner of the globe figured out that pigments from the earth could be mixed into a paste and applied to a surface, almost instantly transforming it. Unfortunately, many of the raw materials were costly and rare and thus only available to the wealthy in the past. Today we are enjoying a virtual renaissance of many of the tradi-

tional techniques used to decorate surfaces throughout the ages. And luckily, with technology has come a veritable rainbow of colors that are inexpensive and readily available. Thanks to the development of water-based paints and varnishes, it's easy for anyone to learn techniques that were undertaken only by skilled artisans in the past.

If the abundance of paint products on the market is any indication, it is safe to say that people love color. And if the evidence that Neanderthal man was buried with ocher pigment is any indication, it's also valid to say that people have *always* been attracted by its power. Although it's believed that man began painting objects before developing the

A painted trinket box, left, decorated by an early nineteenth-century artist, continues to delight today.

14

skill to paint pictures, our ancestors were scratching images on cave walls with tinted pigment as early as the Stone Age.

Early artists didn't actually have paint as we know it, however. Instead, they discovered that ground minerals such as black manganese ore, iron, and copper could be mixed with animal fat or egg white to produce a paste with which they could apply color to a surface. Whatever was available in a region literally set the tone for that place. For example, umber was abundant in a part of Italy now called Umbria. Likewise, the region of Sienna produced the pigment known by the same name.

Today, the paint we use to apply color or create images can be defined simply as an emulsion consisting of three ingredients: pigment, binder, and thinner. *Pigment* gives paint its color. Until the development of synthetic coal-tar-based aniline dyes in Germany during the 1850s, all pigments were derived from natural sources that were ground into fine powders. Today's chemical dyes tend to be brighter and harsher than natural colors, but they do come in a wider range of shades and tones than the natural ones.

A *binder* is a heavy liquid that glues pigments together so that they can adhere to a surface. There are two types of binders in interior paints: latex and alkyd. A *thinner* is a substance that can be used to dilute a mixture of pigment and binder to make it spreadable.

An antique, polychrome-decorated, marbled overmantel mirror, above, was done in the Italian Baroque style.

Painted Faux Finishes

Throughout its evolution, paint has been used to serve many practical and aesthetic purposes, including decoration, protection, preservation, camouflage, and simulation of other materials. The fascination with *faux* (the French word for false) finishes has endured since the ancient Myceans painted pottery to resemble marble. Historically, there are many reasons for substituting an imitation for the real thing. Take marble, for example. While marble is quarried in a vast array of colors and textures, many types are rare and costly, extremely heavy to transport, and difficult to work with. It's easy to understand why Renaissance architects hired painters to create faux versions in churches both humble and grand. The Sistine Chapel and Saint Peter's Basilica in Rome each contain fine examples of the technique.

Graining, or the painting of surfaces to resemble wood, dates back to ancient Egypt. Wood was rare and highly valued in Egypt. Graining was a way to create the look of wood without paying a fortune. In Europe, graining has gone in and out of favor since Medieval times and was often used simply as a way of making a poorer quality wood, such as pine, resemble a finer one, such as rosewood. This enabled the merchant class to acquire

furniture that resembled what only royalty could afford.

European techniques were brought to America by immigrant artisans in the early eighteenth century. By the early nineteenth century, itinerant painters traveled from town to town, spreading the decorative wealth by

The grain-painted seed chest, above, attributed to a nineteenth-century American artisan, was made in Lancaster County, Pennsylvania.

Another faux wood finish distinguishes an antique récamier, left, made in New York between the years 1815 and 1825.

applying painted finishes to the walls, doors, floors, and furnishings of Colonial homes.

Painted Furniture

We know that the ancient Egyptians painted much of their furniture, thanks to beautifully preserved examples found in their tombs. Egyptian artisans applied several coats of a sealant (similar to gesso) to wood and then rubbed on pigmented stains, often adding gilded accents. Fragments of Chinese hand-painted lacquered objects survive from as early as 206 B.C. But the real golden age of furniture painting began in the seventeenth century with the European fascination for Oriental lacquerware. The Queen of Siam presented Louis XIV with a gift of two pieces and started a major trend.

True lacquering, a time-consuming process involving the application of many coats of a sumac-based shellac, produces a highly polished surface. The characteristic background colors of red, from cinnabar, and black, from charred bone meal, were painstakingly decorated with images of fruit, flowers, or pastoral scenes.

Trade routes from the East to the West were responsible for the transport of ideas as well as merchandise, and both traders and travelers brought back exquisite examples of lacquerware from the

Far East sparking an interest in all things Oriental among the European rulers and gentry. When the demand exceeded the supply, European craftsman began to develop simplified methods of lacquering. Perfected by a Frenchman named Martin, the technique was known as *vernis Martin.*

While the interest in Orientalia thrived in the courts, everyday craftsmen were producing their

Italian neoclassic, polychrome-decorated, scarlet and gilt-japanned side tables, above, exemplify European artistry.

own genre of painted furniture influenced by the decorative arts of the Middle Ages and Renaissance. Distinct painting styles developed in different regions. In Russia, Switzerland, and Scandinavia, stylized interpretations of local flora applied to simple furniture painted in strong colors became the basis of what we now call "folk art painting." Less technically complex than laquerware, this

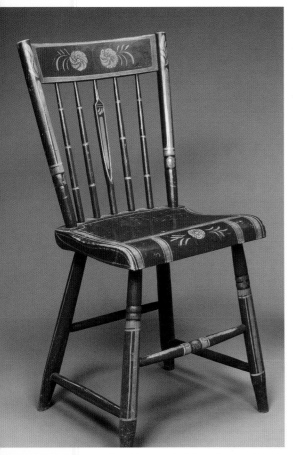

This painted and decorated fancy side chair, left, is an example of early nineteenth-century craftsmanship.

A small, antique Pennsylvania chest, below, features a compass-drawn design.

This painted blanket chest, bottom, is from the late eighteenth or early nineteenth century.

type of painted furniture became more available to the masses as itinerant painters traveled around offering their services as door-to-door decorators, often in exchange for room and board only.

AMERICAN PAINTED FURNITURE

This tradition continued in America where regional styles developed, as well. Early settlers usually brought few pieces of furniture to this country, so the impulse was to create a decorative object reminiscent of their

homeland. Initially, styles were distinct to a particular area, but as traveling painters brought ideas from one place to another, America became more of a decorative melting pot.

The advent of manufactured furniture in the late nineteenth century brought a decline in production and interest in painted furniture. With the exception of the Arts and Crafts Movement and the Aesthetic Movement, which produced some fine examples of painted furniture, few attempts were made to preserve the traditional techniques. Today's renewed fascination with painted finishes serves both an aesthetic and an historic purpose.

Decoupage

Decoupage, from the French verb *decouper*, meaning to cut out, refers to the technique of applying cut-out paper to an object or wall. The notion of applying paper to surfaces is probably as old as paper itself, which was developed in second-century China. A few rare examples of early Chinese and Persian decoupage pieces have survived. The technique was used widely by monks in the Middle Ages, who applied hand-painted papers to the walls of their monasteries and decorated small objects with finely engraved papers.

The real heyday of the technique, though, wasn't until the seventeenth century, when

A Victorian table, below left, features papier-mâché: wet paper that is shaped, and then painted and varnished when dry.

A nineteenth-century crafter decorated these hat boxes, below, with wallpaper.

decoupage was used to replicate the look of hand-painted lacquerware by covering paper applied to a painted surface with many coats of varnish to create a smooth transparent finish. This was a way of further simplifying the production of the popular lacquer look. While the Asians did use paper cutouts on some of their objects, it was the Europeans who really developed decoupage into an art form. In Italy, the application of paper images to furniture was called *arte del povervo*, or poor man's art, since it mimicked the look of hand painting but was much less costly to produce. Apprentices would hand paint black-and-white prints with oil paints, then apply these images to painted furniture. Up to 15 coats of varnish disguised the fact that the image was applied paper and not actually hand painted. Much sanding and rubbing was done between coats to ensure a completely smooth finish.

VICTORIAN DECOUPAGE

Highly popular again in Victorian times with both ladies and gentlemen of leisure, decoupage was done with a variety of paper goods to create complex collages on boxes, trunks, folding screens, and just about everything else! The availability of mass-produced printed and embossed papers opened up infinite possibilities for surface design. Themes included cherubs, animals, fruits, and flowers. Typical Victorian pieces were layered with a range of images from scrapbook cutouts and paper dolls to botanical drawings and gold paper braid. Even Queen Victoria herself enjoyed the art of decoupage and was an avid collector of unique examples. Victorian decoupage is probably epitomized by the magnificent scrap screens and trunks. Folding screens, either room-sized or for the tabletop,

and leather trunks and traveling cases were richly adorned with colored scrapbook images.

The art of decoupage has gone in and out of fashion over the years and is today flourishing again, probably due in part to the development of non-yellowing, water-based top coats.

Stenciling

Stenciling, also Chinese in origin, was originally done on fabric. Early stencils were created by placing a

An authentic example of Early American stenciling exists in this home as part of an exhibit of historic buildings and artifacts on display at the Shelburne Museum in Shelburne, Vermont.

This green-painted and gilt-stenciled side table was made in Baltimore during the early nineteenth century.

series of pinpricks into a toughened paper or leaf. Powdered charcoal rubbed over the design left the impression of the image on the fabric. As the technique evolved, a simple design was cut from stiff paper with a sharp knife. This template was laid on the surface to be decorated, and color was applied with a brush, sponge, or rag—essentially how it is still done today. The beauty of this simple concept is that it allows the artist to repeat a motif over and over again. Similar techniques were developed almost simultaneously by the Egyptians, the ancient Romans, the Japanese, the Persians, and the Eskimos of the Baffin Islands. Stenciling as we know it was brought to Europe along trade routes during the early days of Christianity. Charlemagne stenciled his initials onto important documents. Early stencils were used to make playing cards and in combination with woodcuts to illustrate early books. During the Middle Ages, especially in Britain, monks stenciled images onto the walls of churches using pigment and gold leaf. In fact, it is thought that the word stencil derives from the Middle French word *estanceler,* meaning to sparkle. The French began to make stenciled wallpaper in the early seventeenth century, and for the next 200 years stenciling was widely used in Europe.

STENCILING IN AMERICA

Today many people think of stenciling as an American art form and, indeed, stenciling really flourished in Colonial America. With a simple template and a bit of paint, the effect of wallpaper could be achieved, a plain floor was refined, or a length of canvas was transformed into a carpet. Revived in recent years as a facet of the interest in country decorating, stenciling today need not be limited to a rustic look. Stencils can add interest to any style of design no matter how simple or sophisticated it might be.

Just as seventeenth-century European craftsmen found ways to simplify Oriental lacquering methods, today's artists are using newer paints and glazes to simplify all kinds of techniques. Inspired by tradition and benefiting from technology, the history of decorative finishes continues to evolve.

Preparation & Equipment

Not having a well-equipped basement workshop shouldn't discourage you from doing any of the projects in this book. While it's important to have a clean, well-ventilated space with good lighting, you can set up a temporary work area in an unused corner, in part of the garage, or even in the backyard. Wherever it is, you'll need a work surface. If you decide to transform your kitchen or dining room, protect the table with several layers of brown kraft paper. Some hardware stores carry it in big sheets that can be used as drop cloths. If you can't find sheets, the paper is widely available rolled on a tube. After covering the table with paper, spread a clear plastic tarp over that, and secure it with masking tape. When the plastic gets messy, as it surely will, replace it with another sheet.

Planning ahead is the key to completing a project quickly. Take inventory of what you'll need before you even begin. There is nothing more frustrating than having to stop your work to run out to the hardware store for steel wool because you assumed that you already had some. At the end of this chapter is a shopping list of general materials.

Paint is basic to most techniques. Glass dessert dishes, small mixing bowls, or plastic storage containers are all ideal for mixing paint. Save the plastic lidded containers from salad bars. They provide a clever solution to the problem of paint drying up when you can't finish something in one session. When you've completed a project, return any unused paint to its original package or store it in a tightly sealed container. When working with small amounts of multiple colors, use a palette. If you don't have an artist's watercolor palette, coated paper plates make good disposable substitutes. When mixing a new shade of paint, always save a small amount to use for touching up any imperfections that may occur before you apply the sealer coat. Bamboo chopsticks and tongue depressors make good mixing sticks for stirring small amounts of paint. The paint sticks given out at hardware stores are fine for stirring large quantities.

Without a doubt, the most important tools for applying painted finishes are, of course, brushes. **Paintbrushes** vary widely in both quality and price. Traditional professional paint finishes often involve labor-intensive, multiple-step techniques and oil- or shellac-based ingredients, which are difficult to work with. In addition, the special tools and brushes needed for many of these methods are an investment in themselves. This book tries to keep materials and steps simple so that you don't have to spend $100 for a badger brush when a $10 soft bristle brush will suffice. It's a good idea to purchase several good **artist's brushes**, **stencil brushes** in a couple

of sizes, a **dragging brush**, and a **stippler**, a **spatter brush**, and **liner**, **pointed**, and **round brushes**. (Also see page 24.)

Disposable **foam brushes** are a fabulous innovation with numerous advantages, including their low cost. Foam brushes don't leave brush marks on your work, and there's no risk of bristles falling out and getting stuck in the wet paint. They do have limitations, though, so don't attempt to use them for absolutely everything. For example, on surfaces with many crevices, **bristle brushes** will provide the best overall coverage. Also, foam brushes wear out quickly and must be replaced

Assorted paintbrushes

Fine brushes

Artist's brushes

Dragging brush

Foam brushes

often, which probably explains why they are available by the bagful!

Always keep a supply of old towels and soft cotton rags around. They come in handy for both cleaning up and applying some techniques. Also keep paper towels, **sponges**, and clean water close at hand. If there isn't a sink in your work area, keep a bucket of water on the floor nearby.

A **pencil** or, better yet, a chalk pencil is good for marking the placement of motifs or images. Chalk lines can be wiped off easily, which lets you make changes without ruining the base coat or the background finish.

Many projects and techniques require working one section at a time. Cover the adjacent sections with low-tack **masking tape** to protect them from paints. For a large area, tape a sheet of paper over the surface.

You can also use masking tape or a ruler to mark guidelines to keep motifs straight or level. Use a **craft knife** if you have to cut the masking tape around shapes or corners. Burnish the edges of the tape to keep paints from seeping underneath. Afterward, carefully remove the masking tape before the paint is thoroughly dry. Touch up any fuzzy edges with a fine paintbrush.

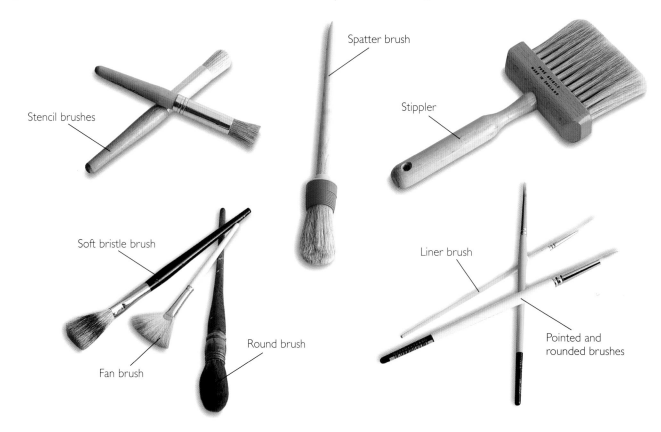

Stencil brushes

Spatter brush

Stippler

Soft bristle brush

Fan brush

Round brush

Liner brush

Pointed and rounded brushes

Wooden objects will generally require sanding or smoothing before finishes are applied. If there is an existing finish on the surface, remove any loose or flaking portions. Avoid using furniture that needs to be stripped unless you're adamant about it and don't mind applying elbow grease to this extra step. In that case, carefully follow the manufacturer's instructions for the stripping agent you select, and wear sturdy **gloves** and a **mask** while working (page 26). Wash really dirty items with trisodium phosphate (TSP), which is available at hardware stores, and a **scrub brush**. Allow everything to dry completely before sanding or painting. Fill in holes and cracks with wood putty as necessary. Sand down the surface with three grades of **sandpaper**. You may want to use an electric sander on large flat surfaces. Begin with a coarse grade of 60- or 100-grit sandpaper and finish with a finer grade of 150- or 200-grit sandpaper. Always wipe with tack cloths after sanding.

Most of the projects and techniques featured in this book are done with latex **primers**, **paints**, and **glazes**, which are easier to work with, faster-drying, and environmentally safer than their oil-based counterparts (page 26). These products have the added advantage of easy clean up. You can quickly clean brushes loaded with latex paint with warm water. For brushes that have

Kitchen sponges

Natural bristle scrub brush

Natural sponge

Tweezers

Masking tape and painter's tapes

Ruler

Craft knife

Pencil

been used with oil-based paints, you'll have to first clean them with paint thinner, then wash them out with mild soap and warm water.

Most surfaces will need at least one coat of primer before painting with the base color. Use a good-quality, multipurpose latex primer. This will ensure that the paint will adhere to the surface rather than soak into it. Next, cover the surface with one or two coats of the base color. For certain projects, a heavy-duty, shellac-based primer is recommended to camouflage really stubborn stains and knots. In some cases, the wood grain is meant to show through. These items don't require priming. Always use a metal primer on

metal objects, following the manufacturer's instructions for preparing the surface and application. If the piece is rusty, go over it with a scraper, wire brush, or **steel wool** prior to priming. When working with spray paints, it's especially important to keep the work place well ventilated. Some people prefer to use spray paint outdoors only, but wind can make doing so difficult.

A glaze adds depth and richness to a base color. By definition, a glaze will always be translucent no matter how dark the shade is. Traditionally, glazes were always oil-based and usually involved a time-consuming multiple application process to achieve depth and richness. In recent years, water-based

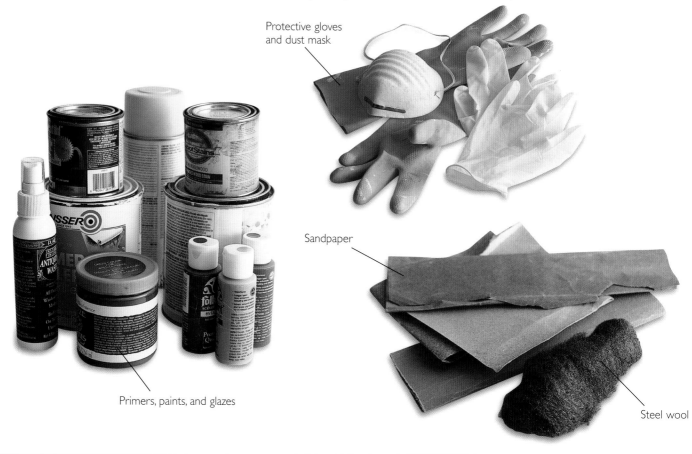

Protective gloves and dust mask

Sandpaper

Primers, paints, and glazes

Steel wool

glazes have been developed that fairly successfully mimic the look obtained by oil glazing. While they don't give the same rich patina a true oil-based glaze would, premixed acrylic glazes are used here for some projects. If you prefer to create your own, mix acrylic paints with a neutral glaze and a thinner until you get the shade you desire.

When trying a new technique especially with **combs**, **stencils**, **stamps**, or **sponges**, practice on a sanded board before actually beginning the project. A 16-inch square of plywood is an ideal surface that is still a manageable size, but large enough to really show the effect of the technique.

If you don't have access to a table saw, most lumberyards will cut a sheet of plywood into squares for you.

Some techniques require manipulation while the paint or glaze is still wet. Do these one section at a time. Keep the outside edge wet so that you can smoothly feather it into the next section without creating a hard break or line in the finish.

Allow the paints to dry before proceeding on to the next step unless otherwise noted. When stenciling, do not reposition your stencil or work on another section before the paint is dry to the touch in order to prevent smudges or smears.

Rubber stamps and foam shapes

Stencils

Plastic combs

Some projects, such as decoupage, don't use paint at all but instead use **art papers**, **wallcoverings**, or **wrapping paper**. For these you need **scissors**, **decoupage medium** (a kind of adhesive), and foam brushes.

Certain projects in this book include highlighting or adding an antique effect. They will require working with **liquid gold**, **liquid gilding**, **gold wax**, or **metal leaf**. In most cases, your aim will be to apply a bit of faded glory rather than all-out glitz, so don't worry about creating a smooth, even coat. If it looks worn, it's all the better.

On wooden pieces you can go over the finish with a **cheesecloth** and **furniture wax**. Other projects may call for "aging" wood with **antiquing wax**, **shoe polish**, or **candle wax**.

When your project—paint or otherwise—is completed, seal it with two or more coats of a water-based product. (Always allow paints to dry for 24 hours in order to cure completely before applying a sealer to the finish.)

Shopping List

In addition to specific brushes and materials required for each technique, stock these supplies:

KRAFT PAPER

CLEAR PLASTIC DROP CLOTH

Art papers for decoupage

Wallcoverings, borders, and wrapping papers

Decoupage tools: scissors, decoupage medium, and foam brush

WOOD PUTTY OR WOOD FILLER

SANDPAPER: 3 DIFFERENT GRADES

STEEL WOOL

TACK CLOTHS

MULTIPURPOSE PRIMER

HEAVY-DUTY PRIMER

MINERAL SPIRITS

SPONGES: NATURAL AND CELLULOSE

MASKING OR PAINTER'S TAPE

CRAFT KNIFE

PLASTIC OR GLASS MIXING
CONTAINERS IN ASSORTED SIZES

MIXING STICKS

PAINT PALETTES OR
COATED PAPER PLATES

PAPER TOWELS

NEWSPAPER

SOFT LINT-FREE CLOTHS
(SUCH AS OLD COTTON T-SHIRTS)

PENCILS

RULER OR STRAIGHTEDGE

MEASURING TAPE

LARGE MULTIPURPOSE AND
SMALL SHARP POINTED SCISSORS

ACRYLIC SEALER IN
SATIN OR GLOSS FINISH

Liquid gold

Liquid gilding

Gold wax

Metal leaf

Cheesecloth

Furniture wax

Candle wax

Antiquing wax

Shoe polish

Finishes & Techniques

The simplest finish can elevate an object from mundane to sublime. The techniques used in this book are, for the most part, so easy that they can be done by a complete novice. The philosophy behind them is "Process, not perfection." The overall effect is more important than the perfection of every detail.

Basic Surfaces

All of these procedures are fun and quick ways to create texture on either small or large areas. They can be used to create backgrounds for other techniques, such as stenciling or decoupage, or they can stand on their own. While they have been applied to furniture and accessories in this book, any of these treatments can be done on walls, as well. Notice how the ragged walls in the chapter "A Child's Room" complement the projects and add a richness to the room. The introduction of texture to a surface, whether it's intended to cover an entire wall or adorn the smallest accessory, adds depth and visual interest that draws the eye in.

With some of these treatments, you add texture by applying paint or glaze with a brush or bunched-up cloth, allowing some of the base coat to show through. In others, such as dragging and frottage, you take some of the wet top coat away to expose the base coat; these are called "subtractive" techniques.

Using contrasting colors for the base and top coats produces a stronger look than using related shades. Buy a premixed glaze in any color, or make a glaze yourself using acrylic paint and a colorless glazing medium. Experiment with the amounts until you get the desired translucent shade.

COLOR WASHING

YOU WILL NEED: Acrylic paint for base coat • Acrylic paint for top coat • Glazing medium • Flat foam paintbrushes • 3-inch flat bristle paintbrush • Mixing container • OPTIONAL: Third color

Using a flat brush, paint the surface with two coats of the base color, and allow it to dry. Mix the glaze. Apply it to the surface with a bristle brush, making random, uneven strokes. Work across the piece in

Apply the top-coat using a flat brush to make random cross-hatched strokes that overlap.

vertical sections. Move the brush down each section making short, overlapping passes in a zigzag pattern *(photo above)*. This builds up a textured crosshatch design with the base coat showing through. You can use additional colors with subsequent coats of glaze, but allow each coat to dry before applying the next one, or the colors will blend together.

COMBING

YOU WILL NEED: Acrylic paint for base coat • Mixed acrylic glaze • Multipurpose rubber paint comb • Flat foam paintbrushes • Paper towels • Stiff cardboard • Scissors or craft knife • Straightedge or ruler

Paint the surface with the base coat, and allow it to dry; then apply one coat of the glaze to cover it *(step 1)*. Glaze one small section at a time if the surface area is large because you have to apply the technique while the glaze is still wet.

To work this technique, hold the comb at an angle of about 80 degrees. Apply enough pressure so that the comb bends slightly and cuts through the wet glaze as you pull it toward you in the desired pattern *(step 2)*. Work wavy or straight lines to create different effects. Go over vertically combed lines with a horizontal pass of the tool for a checkered pattern. Whatever pattern you choose, always keep the comb strokes smooth and steady as you go along. Wipe the comb clean after each pass to off-load excess paint. The uneven edges of the tines and the intervals between them will create different textures. If

1 Apply glaze over the dry base coat. On large surfaces, work one small section at a time.

2 Hold the comb at an 80-degree angle, and drag it through the wet glaze toward you. Make curved or straight lines, but keep strokes smooth and steady.

31

you make a mistake while the glaze is still wet, apply another coat and try again.

If you don't want to purchase the combing tool, you can make a comb from cardboard. Cut a rectangle of stiff cardboard that is approximately 4 inches wide. Notch it with a zigzag pattern along one of the long sides of the rectangle to create tines. Homemade cardboard combs get soggy after a while, so you may need to make several. But if you are painting multiple objects or a moderately large surface, it is worth investing in a rubber comb. For a very large area, such as a wall, try using a notched squeegee. Cut tines to a desired size with a craft knife.

CRACKLE GLAZING

YOU WILL NEED: Acrylic paint for base coat • Acrylic paint for top coat • Crackle medium • Antiquing medium • Paintbrushes • Soft lint-free cloth

Go over the surface with two coats of the base color, and allow it to dry. This is the paint color that will show between the cracks when the technique is completed and has thoroughly dried. It should contrast pleasingly with the color of the top coat you choose. Using a brush, apply one coat of the crackle medium in smooth strokes, covering the entire surface of your project in one pass *(step 1)*. Do not coat the same area twice. Keep in mind, the thicker the coat of crackle medium, the wider the cracks will be. Vary the thickness over the surface for the random look of natural aging. Brushing on the medium in vari-

1 Brush on one coat of crackle medium. For wide cracks, apply a thick coat; for a subtler affect, use a thin layer of the liquid.

2 Before the crackle medium becomes thoroughly dry, apply the contrasting top coat.

3 The final finish. To accentuate the cracks, rub antiquing medium into them using a soft rag.

ous directions will form a more complex and interesting pattern, as well. When the crackle medium is almost—but not thoroughly—dry, apply one coat of the contrasting paint over the surface *(step 2)*. As it dries, you'll notice that it curls back in spots to reveal the base-coat color *(step 3)*. An optional finishing technique is to rub antiquing medium over the cracks using a soft rag. Wipe away any excess, leaving just enough to lightly highlight the cracks.

DISTRESSING

YOU WILL NEED: Candle wax • Acrylic paint for the top coat • Antiquing wax or brown shoe polish • Sandpaper • Steel wool • Tack cloths • Flat foam paintbrushes • Soft lint-free cloths

This finish works well on both unfinished and finished wood. Remove any surface imperfections using fine sandpaper or steel wool. The candle wax serves as a resister, preventing the areas it covers from absorbing paint. Rub it onto selected places

1 After sanding the surface to a smooth finish, rub candle wax into any areas where you want to simulate natural wear. Typically, this should be near the edges or at the corners.

on the surface *(step 1)*. Choose spots that would most naturally become exposed to wear over time, such as near the edges and on and around the corners and knobs. Cover the entire surface with one coat of paint, and allow it to dry *(step 2)*. Then, with the sandpaper or steel wool, go over the waxed areas to lift off some of the paint *(step 3)*. To intensify the illusion of age, rub the entire surface with a coat of antiquing wax. Apply a little extra in the "worn" spots, scuffing it a bit with a piece of steel wool

2 Apply one coat of acrylic paint to cover the entire surface. Let it dry thoroughly.

3 With steel wool or sandpaper, go back over the waxed areas to scratch off the new paint.

4 Rub in a small amount of brown shoe polish or antiquing wax into the "worn" spots. Use steel wool to scuff it.

(step 4). If you don't have antiquing medium, an excellent substitute is brown shoe polish.

DRAGGING

YOU WILL NEED: Acrylic paint for the base coat • Acrylic glaze • Dragging brush or stiff-bristled whisk broom • Flat foam paintbrushes

Paint the surface with two coats of the base color, and allow it to dry. Because the dragging technique must be worked on wet glaze, it is a good idea to work in small sections if the overall surface is large. With that in mind, apply one coat of the glaze *(step 1)*. Hold the handle of the dragging brush at a 45-degree angle above the surface, and pull the bristles through the glaze toward you *(step 2)*. (For larger surfaces, you can use a good-quality, stiff-bristled whisk broom.) Drag the brush slowly and steadily, making one uninterrupted pass. Continue onto the next section, overlapping with the wet edge of the previous one so as not to create a distinct break in the finish. The lines you make do not have to be perfectly straight. The charm of the technique is that it is supposed to look as if it was done by hand. Usually, the lines are vertical, but they can be horizontal, diagonal, or curved, as well. Make them fine or bold. Create combed, plaited, or crosshatched patterns. For success, the dragging brush must remain relatively dry at all times. When it starts to collect paint, wash and dry it before continuing.

1 After the base coat dries thoroughly, apply one coat of glaze over the surface.

2 Hold the handle of the dragging brush at a 45-degree angle above the surface, and pull the bristles through the wet glaze toward you.

FROTTAGE

YOU WILL NEED: Acrylic paint for base coat • Acrylic paint for top coat • Newspapers or plastic wrap • Flat foam paintbrushes • Mixing container

Apply two or more base coats, and allow the paint to dry. In the meantime, make a wash of one part paint (using the paint intended for the top coat) and two parts water. The mixture should be the consistency of milk. Because acrylic paint dries quickly and the technique requires a wet surface, work in small sections. First, apply the wash *(step 1)*. Take a large sheet of newspaper, and smooth it over the wet paint. Some newspaper ink comes off easily; if that is the case, use newsprint paper or plain brown wrapping paper. Using your fingers or the palms of your hands, push the paper around in the wet paint to create a pattern *(step 2)*. Immediately, pull the paper off the wet paint *(step 3)*. Go on to the next section. With each one, change the direction in which you remove the paper to add more complexity to the painted texture's appearance. If you are working on a small object or where there are curves or corners, you can substitute plastic wrap, which fits easily into tight spaces and crevices, for the newspaper. Wrinkles and creases in the paper or plastic wrap are desirable and actually enhance the textural look of the finished technique. Paper will absorb some of the thinned paint, but plastic wrap won't, so the effect produced by the two materials will be slightly different.

1 Apply the wash to a small section of the surface over a thoroughly dry base coat or two of paint.

2 Smooth a large sheet of newspaper over the wet paint. Push the paint around with the palm of your hand or your fingers.

3 Immediately lift off the newspaper. Don't wait for the paint to become dry.

RAGGING

YOU WILL NEED: Acrylic paint for the base coat • Acrylic glaze for the top coat • Flat foam paint-brushes • Soft lint-free cloths

Paint the surface with two coats of the base color, and allow it to dry. This is another technique that requires a wet top coat of glaze, so divide the surface or object into sections that you can work on one at a time. First, apply a contrasting coat of glaze over the

1 With a flat foam brush, apply a contrasting colored glaze over a thoroughly dry base coat.

2 Use a bunched-up soft cloth to lift off some of the glaze. Keep turning the cloth to avoid creating an obvious pattern.

base coat *(step 1)*. Do not worry about consistent brush strokes, as the ragging will work the glaze. Next, press a bunched-up piece of cloth into the wet glaze *(step 2)*. Move the cloth around in different directions to avoid creating a discernible pattern. Change to a clean cloth frequently. Don't continue to use a cloth when it has become engorged with glaze. The idea is to lift off glaze, exposing some of the base-coat color.

PAINTING STRIPES AND PLAID

YOU WILL NEED: Acrylic or latex paint for the base coat • Acrylic paint for the stripes • Flat foam paintbrushes • Fine artist's paintbrush: medium round • Sponge: natural or cellulose • Masking tape • Craft knife • Chalk pencil • Ruler or straightedge

Apply two base coats, and allow them to dry. The success of this technique depends largely on what you do before you begin to paint it. Measure the surface of the project, and then divide it into evenly distributed stripes. Mark their placement with a chalk pencil; then run a strip of masking tape along the outside edge of each one. To make the job easier, use masking tape that is the same width as the stripes, if possible. Smooth the tape down and burnish the edges with your fingers to secure it in place. Use a small piece of sponge or a foam brush to pull the paint over the unmasked area *(step 1)*. When the paint is thoroughly dry, remove the tape. *Voilà,*

1 After carefully measuring and masking, use a sponge or a foam brush to paint stripes.

2 Paint new stripes across the first ones to create a crossbarred pattern. Use the same color and stripe width for a checked plaid or various colors and widths for a traditional tartan look.

stripes! Creating a plaid design entails an additional step. Working perpendicular to the stripes you have just painted, mark new ones that can be the same or a different width as the originals. After masking the outside edges, paint the new stripes, which will intersect the first ones to form a crossbarred design *(step 2)*. Use the same color paint or a contrasting one. When the new paint dries thoroughly, remove the tape *(step 3)*.

3 After the paint is completely dry, remove the tape. You can touch up any uneven edges with a fine artist's brush, or leave them as is.

Hand Painting

You do not have to be an expert painter to experiment with some of the simple hand-painted motifs in this book. A delicate hand-painted border adds a special, one-of-a-kind quality to a finish and gives your work a professional appearance when it is combined with a decorative paint technique. It's worth spending some time experimenting with different artist's brushes on paper or on a wooden board until you become comfortable enough to add some unique detailing to one of your projects.

SIMPLE HAND PAINTING

YOU WILL NEED: Acrylic paint in various colors • Fine artist's brushes, including flat, liner, pointed, and round in assorted sizes • Pencil • Sponge • Paper towels • Transfer paper

The most important advice about hand painting is to use high-quality artist's brushes. Cheap ones lose bristles and leave brush marks. Always practice on a board or paper before painting on the real surface *(step 1)*. Begin by marking the placement for the design and drawing it lightly with a pencil. Or you can use transfer paper to trace patterns from this book that you can carry over the surface or object you are decorating. Position the traced motif in place on your project, and slip a piece of transfer paper between the motif and the project. Retrace the lines of the motif, using a ball-point pen to transfer it onto your project. Using an artist's flat or round paintbrush and the colors of your choice, dip the brush into the paint, and then dab off a bit of the paint. Gently guide the brush, allowing it to do the work, pressing down and easing up to vary the thickness of the line *(step 2)*. Always keep a damp sponge and paper towels handy for quick cleanup. If you make a mistake, wipe off the paint quickly and try again.

HAND PAINTING FROM A STENCIL

YOU WILL NEED: Assorted acrylic paint colors • Stencil brushes • Stencils • Ball-point pen • Spray adhesive • Fine artist's brushes: 1-inch flat, medium liner, medium round, #2 or #3 pointed • Paper towels • Chalk pencils • Ruler or straightedge

Paint the object or surface in any desired finish coat, and allow it to dry. Position the stencil on the surface to be decorated using spray adhesive to hold it in place. For extra support, tape it down. Using a pencil, trace

1 It's an excellent idea to practice on a board before attempting to hand paint a design on the actual surface or object you are decorating.

2 After lightly drawing or transferring a traced design onto your surface, allow the brush to do the work. Press down or ease up to vary the thickness of the lines.

1 After mounting the stencil, trace the outlines of the design onto the object or surface you wish to paint.

2 Use an artist's brush to create shading on your design. This will give your work a professional appearance.

the outlines of the stencil's shapes *(step 1)*. Once you've traced the entire design, remove the stencil template. Even though you will not paint the design entirely freehand, it's a good idea to practice on a board before attempting the real thing. This way, you can make brush strokes and create shading with confidence later.

Using artist's flat and round paintbrushes and the colors of your choice, fill in the outlined areas of the motif *(step 2)*. Double- or triple-load a flat paintbrush with different shades of color to add dimension. Use a stencil brush and a small amount of paint to create texture or a blush of color.

Stenciling

Stenciling is an excellent method for creating a repetitive pattern on a surface. Historically, it was the way middle-class people imitated the look of wallpaper, which once could be afforded only by the priviledged classes.

Most people are familiar with what is called "positive stenciling." The motif to be applied is typically cut into acetate or stencil paper. This cut-out image acts as a template; paint is applied inside the cut-out areas to transfer the image to a surface, such as a wall or a piece of furniture. With "negative stenciling," instead of painting inside a cut-out shape, you paint around it. Remove the template, and the outline of the image remains on the surface.

POSITIVE STENCILING

YOU WILL NEED: Acrylic paints in assorted colors • Stencil blanks or paper • Stencil brushes • Tracing paper • Spray adhesive • Flat foam paintbrushes • Masking or painter's tape • Craft knife • Paper towels • Pencil • Ruler or straightedge

Paint the surface with two coats of the base color, and allow it to dry. Spray the reverse side of the stencil with spray adhesive to keep it from slipping while working. Position the template where you want the image to appear, and tape it in place. Dip the stencil brush into the paint, and then blot it on

1 Blot excess paint onto a paper towel to keep lines crisp. The key to expert stenciling is to use a tiny amount of paint.

a paper towel *(step 1)*. The only trick involved with stenciling is to use a small amount of paint.

Stencil with one color of paint at a time. Mask any areas you are not working on. Pounce the brush up and down to make crisp, clean edges *(step 2)*. Work from the edges toward the center. You may blend the colors as you desire. Use lighter colors toward the center of the design, and make them darker toward the outside of the shape. You can create a hard edge or fade the paint into the back-ground color. Use less paint, and build up layers for a clean professional-quality finish.

Always use a clean brush or a separate one for each color of paint you apply to your design *(step 3)*. Wipe off any excess paint from the template to prevent undesirable smears and smudges on your surface. Vary the direction of your motifs by reversing your stencil or positioning it at different angles. Let each layer of paint dry before applying another one.

2 With the template securely in place, pounce on the paint using quick, stacatto movements.

3 Work from the edges to inside the cut-out area, and always use a clean brush to apply each new color.

MAKING YOUR OWN STENCIL

Trace or photocopy the image you want to stencil, reducing or enlarging as needed. Spray the back of the paper with the image on it with spray adhesive, and adhere it to the stencil paper. Place stencil paper and the design on a clean, level surface, and cut out the design using a sharp craft knife. If you make a mistake, don't attempt to cut the same line again. Cut a new line to ensure clean, even edges. Move the stencil around as you cut, so you are always cutting at an angle that gives you the most control over the blade.

NEGATIVE STENCILING

YOU WILL NEED: Acrylic paint for a base coat • Contrasting color of spray paint • Desired distinctive flat shapes (such as leaf or fern) • Spray adhesive • Flat foam paintbrushes

Paint the surface with two coats of the base color, and allow it to dry. The base coat will be the color of the stenciled image. Spray the reverse side of your shapes with spray adhesive. Arrange them around

1 Arrange all of the shapes in a pleasing pattern; let some of them partially extend beyond the edges of the surface for a natural look.

2 The final effect. Don't use too much adhesive, or the forms will be difficult to remove after the spray paint has dried.

the surface of your project *(step 1)*. Extend the shapes beyond your work surface to give partial shapes. Do not overlap the shapes, or they will lose their distinctive outlines. Press the shapes in place to keep spray paint from seeping underneath. Work in a well-ventilated space. Cover your work surface to protect it. Following manufacturer's instructions and holding the spray-paint can 2 to 4 feet from the project, spray a fine mist of color onto the surface to cover it completely. Move the spray can back and forth to create

an even and thorough coat. Spraying large amounts of paint will result in drips, so it is best to build up several layers, one at a time. When the paint is dry, remove the shapes *(step 2)*.

Re-creating Nature

In the past, mimicking the look of stone surfaces with paint was a lengthy and often difficult process. As water-based paints and glazes began to replace oil-based products, the techniques became more accessible to the average do-it-yourselfer. Today there are kits on the market that make creating a stone-top table literally as easy as one, two, three.

When you are painting a faux stone, it helps to work from a sample of the real thing. Most stone tile stores will sell you a sample piece. Use this as a guide for colors, shading, and patterning, such as marble veining. Experiment on a board before actually working on the real surface.

MALACHITE

YOU WILL NEED: Pale green acrylic craft paint • Dark green acrylic glaze • Rubber malachite paint comb • Flat foam paintbrushes • Paper towels

Paint the surface with two or more coats of the pale green paint base coat, and allow it to dry. Work one section at a time, as the technique requires that the top coat remain wet in order to manipulate it. With that in mind, apply a coat of the dark green glaze to one section of the surface.

1 After the light-green base coat dries, apply a dark green glaze with a foam brush.

2 With a scrunched up paper towel, lift off some of the wet glaze and smooth over any brush strokes.

3 To create the malachite pattern, hold the comb at an 80-degree angle, and drag it firmly and evenly through the wet glaze, making half-round "petals."

(step 1). Wad up a paper towel, and gently pat the wet surface to remove some of the dark green glaze and to smooth out brush strokes *(step 2)*. Holding the combing tool at an 80-degree angle above the work surface, immediately drag it through the wet glaze. Make wavy, rounded motions, and apply pressure firmly as you cut through the glaze *(step 3)*. Keep your hand strokes smooth and steady as you create a shape that almost looks like the petals of a flower. Overlap the strokes as desired. If you make a mistake while the paint is still wet, just repaint and try again. Wipe the comb clean after each stroke to remove excess paint.

MARBLING

YOU WILL NEED: Four or more shades of acrylic paint, including black and white • Paint extender • Paint thickener • Denatured alcohol • Stippling brush • Spatter brush • Pointed goose feather • Flat foam paintbrushes • Fine artist's paintbrushes: medium round • Natural sponges • Paper towels • Ruler or straightedge

Use a real marble sample as a guide and for inspiration on color and veining patterns. Paint the project with two coats of the base color, and allow it to dry. Swirl circular loops of each of the paint colors and the white and black in your palette *(step 1)*. Swirl lines of thickener and extender over all of the paint. The extender will thin the colors, making them translucent. If the extender makes the paint runny, add thickener to the mixture so that you can work the technique. Gingerly dab the natural sponge into

1 With a marble tile sample nearby as your guide, swirl loops of paint colors on your palette.

2 Using a natural sponge, lightly dab paint onto the surface. Do not completely cover the base coat.

the paint; then lightly apply the color over the surface of the project *(step 2)*. Leave small areas where the base color shows through, resembling the grooves and crevices of natural marble. Combine colors, and overpaint or underpaint areas to mimic depth. Build up the layers, but never completely obscure the base coat in some areas. Change the direction of the sponge often to avoid a repetitious pattern.

Keep your sponges clean of excess paint by washing them often. While the paint is still wet,

dip the spatter brush in denatured alcohol, and tap the handle lightly with a ruler to spatter the surface *(step 3)*. Next, spatter the surface lightly with water, and allow it to sit for a few minutes; then wipe the water lightly with a sponge. This produces liquidlike shapes, creating an interesting realistic pattern.

With a stippling brush, go over the surface to soften and blend some areas. Work the brush in a variety of directions *(step 4)*. Dip the point of the goose feather in the paints; then use it to paint veins over

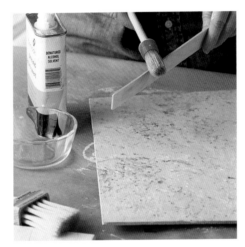

3 Spatter denatured alcohol and water over the paint to make it form unusual, liquidlike patterns.

4 Use the stippling brush in random areas to soften the effect.

5 Using a feather, twirl color onto the surface to create veins.

the surface of the project *(step 5)*. Shaking your hand, twirl the feather while painting to add a more natural appearance. Paint veins in different colors and in different directions. Highlight with a fine paintbrush and contrasting or complementary colors. Soften veins with the stippling brush.

PATINA FINISHING

YOU WILL NEED: Acrylic paints, including turquoise for the base; dark green, antique bronze, or copper for sponging • Flat foam paintbrushes • Fine artist's paintbrushes: medium round • One piece of natural sponge for each color paint • Paper towels

Paint the surface or object with two coats of the turquoise paint (the color of naturally occurring patina), and allow it to dry. Pour the other colors onto your palette. Lightly press the natural sponge into the green paint, and then dab the paint onto the surface *(step 1)*. Leave small areas of the turquoise base coat exposed. For an ideal effect, do not paint

too much at this point; remember, you have to add more colors later. Change the direction of your sponge often to avoid a uniform pattern. Thin some dark green paint with water to create a wash. Using an artist's paintbrush, paint veins over the surface of the project *(step 2)*. Shake your hand, and twirl the paintbrush handle while painting to add a more natural flow. Finally, mottle the appearance by sponging on antique bronze or copper paint *(step 3)*. For realism, leave some areas alone.

1 Dab paint lightly over the object's surface, leaving some of the turquoise base coat exposed.

2 Draw veins over the surface using an artist's brush that has been dipped into a wash made with dark-green paint and water.

3 Mottle the look with random dabs of copper or bronze paint.

Gilding

Traditional gilding requires an adhesive, called gold size, which takes many hours to become tacky enough for the metal leaf to adhere. It then begins to dry immediately, requiring the gilder to work quickly and nimbly. While this method is still used by most professionals, today there is a faster-drying, water-based variety of adhesive (or size) that is preferred by most do-it-yourselfers, who generally lack the time to wait all day to complete a project. The water-based size remains tacky long enough to work the technique, however, so there's no need to worry about speed of execution. Foils are also available; they come in silver, copper, and bronze. Each one produces an elegant look. When first applied, the metal leaf appears garish, but once it's rubbed with wax or shoe polish, it takes on a mellow sheen. Gilded items should be sealed with varnish or shellac so that they won't tarnish.

ANOTHER FAUX STONE TECHNIQUE

Like marble, granite naturally occurs in many distinctive colors and patterns. And, like marble, it is expensive and difficult to install. With some practice, achieving a painted granite look is fairly easy. Borrow or buy some real granite samples, and experiment with painted versions.

GRANITE

YOU WILL NEED: Black acrylic base-coat color, plus several additional shades, including white, green, and bronze or copper • Paint extender • Paint thickener • Fine-holed natural sponges • Flat foam paintbrushes

Paint the project with two or more coats of the black base color, and allow it to dry. It's a good idea to refer to a piece of real granite for authenticity. Swirl circular loops of the additional colors and the white paint in your palette. Swirl some of the thickener and extender over the paint. The extender will thin out the colors; the thickener will keep paint from becoming runny while you work the technique. Lightly dip the natural sponge into the paint palette, and then dab it around on the surface of the project. Combine colors, and apply more or less paint to different areas to vary the depth. While building up layers of paint, allow the black base coat to show through in some places. Change the direction of your sponge often to create a more natural effect.

Use the rubbed gold finish to accent many of the projects. Simply rubbing a bit of golden wax along the edge of something adds a touch of class.

GOLD LEAFING

YOU WILL NEED: Acrylic paint for the base coat • Sheets of imitation gold leaf • Gold size (fast-drying variety) • Antiquing wax or brown shoe polish • Flat foam paintbrushes • Soft natural-bristle paintbrush • Small sheet of thin acetate or gilding tip • Talcum powder • Steel wool • Soft lint-free cloths • Shellac or spray varnish

Work in a dust-free area away from open doors or windows. The sheets of gold leaf are delicate and will fly away in even a slight breeze. Using a foam paintbrush, paint the object with two or more coats of the base color, and allow it to dry *(step 1)*. The base coat will show through the fissures you will create in the gold leaf during the antiquing process later, so choose a color that will contrast well with gold, such as red oxide, terra cotta, dark green, or black. Smooth

1 Apply one or two base coats to the object or surface using a flat foam brush. Choose a color that will contrast well with the gold leaf, such as red oxide.

the surface of your project of any imperfections, such as paint drips, brush streaks, or hairs, with fine sandpaper or steel wool. The gold leaf is thin and will emphasize these imperfections rather than hide them. Gold leaf can be used as an all-over finish on any smooth surface or can be used sparingly as a decorative detail. If the surface or object you are decorating is large, work one small section at a time. Then, using the natural-bristle paintbrush, apply the transparent size *(step 2)*. When the surface feels

2 Apply the adhesive for the gold leaf with a soft, natural-bristle paintbrush; then let it dry to a tacky finish.

3 Use your hands to press the sheets of gold leaf onto the object or surface. Work it into crevices with the soft brush.

4 With a piece of steel wool, rub antiquing wax or brown shoe polish all over the gold leafed surface.

wax to highlight certain areas on a decorated surface. Rub wax onto selected areas of the finished surface using a soft, lint-free cloth or your finger *(see photo, below)*. Work with the grain (if the surface is wood) or with the shape of the form or object.

Use your finger or a soft cloth to apply gold wax to selected areas you wish to highlight.

tacky, cover it by hand with a sheet of the gold leaf *(step 3)*. If you need more than one sheet, you can overlap them. (Dip your fingers in talcum powder so that the gold leaf does not stick to them.) Press the gold leaf into all of the crevices with the natural-bristle brush. You can smooth out the wrinkles and remove any excess by going over the surface of your project with a soft, lint-free cloth. Small cracks in the finish are desirable, however, and will allow the base coat to show through. Finally, rub antiquing wax or brown shoe polish over the entire surface with steel wool to tone it down and enrich the aging effect *(step 4)*.

RUBBING A GOLD FINISH

YOU WILL NEED: Gold wax • Soft, lint-free cloth

This is a finishing technique, so before applying it, make sure the surface you will be working on is clean, dry, and already painted. You can use gold

Decoupage

This technique involves cutting out and pasting images onto a surface, then adding a clear finishing coat. The beauty of both paper and fabric decoupage is that they simulate the look of hand painting without requiring the skill. When rubbed with an antiquing medium, the decoupaged piece takes on a mellow, timeworn appeal. There are endless sources for papers to use, too. Save beautiful wrapping papers, and be on the lookout for more at card stores and museum and book shops. Any copyright-free illustrations from books can be photocopied and used. Old maps, sheet music, and postage stamps are perfect, too.

You can also use wallpaper, as long as it is not too heavy. Thick paper is difficult to burnish, and the edges may keep curling up no matter how many coats of sealer you apply over it.

PAPER DECOUPAGE

YOU WILL NEED: Images from decorative paper or wallpaper • Decoupage medium • Spray adhesive • Steel wool • Flat foam paintbrushes • Pencil • Sharp-pointed scissors • Tweezers • Liquid or spray sealer

Use paper for decoupage on smooth surfaces only. With sharp embroidery scissors, cut out selected images, or motifs *(step 1)*. Include as much or as little of the background of the paper as you wish. In most cases, you should cut most of it away, especially if it clashes with the colors you've chosen for your project. Apply spray adhesive to the reverse side of the images, and then experiment with arranging them on the surface you are decorating. This will hold them in place temporarily until you've selected a final arrangement. You can overlap them to fit around the curves, grooves, or edges, as necessary. Mark the placement lightly with a pencil *(step 2)*. Using a foam brush, coat the reverse side of each image with decoupage medium, working on one piece at a time. Carefully place the motifs on the surface, following the outline you have drawn *(step 3)*. Smooth them down with your fingertips, and work out any air bubbles. Burnish the edges with your fingernail to secure them completely. If you

1 Cut out the images you will apply using sharp scissors that can make fine cuts.

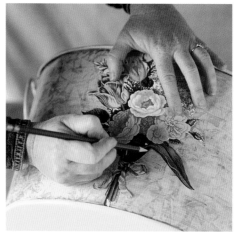

2 When you've decided where you want to apply the image, mark its placement by lightly outlining it on the surface in pencil.

3 Once you have coated the reverse side of the image with decoupage medium, mount it to the surface or object, facing right side up.

4 With the motif in place, apply a layer of decoupage medium to the front of the image and onto the surrounding surface.

are overlapping images, apply them to the surface one at a time. When the design is complete, coat the surface with a layer of decoupage medium *(step 4)*. Let the surface dry, and then go over it with several coats of sealer. Let each coat dry, and then burnish it with steel wool. Apply additional coats of sealer until all of the edges around the motifs are smooth. For smaller projects, you can use a spray sealer.

FABRIC DECOUPAGE

YOU WILL NEED: Images from decorative fabric • Decoupage medium • Flat foam paintbrushes • Craft knife • Pencil • Sharp-pointed scissors • Spray adhesive • Spray sealer, acrylic

Using sharp embroidery scissors, cut out the images. Leave as much or as little of the background as you desire. In most cases, you should cut away the background, especially if it conflicts with the colors chosen to finish the rest of the project. Also, keep in mind that fabric will assume the texture of the surface.

With the cut-out motifs in hand, begin to play with an arrangement. To make this easier, spray the reverse side of the images with spray adhesive. This will temporarily hold them in place until you settle on a permanent arrangement. You can overlap images to fit them around corners. Mark the placement lightly with a pencil. Using a foam brush, coat the wrong side of each motif with decoupage medium *(step 1)*. Work with one piece at a time. Apply the image to the surface *(step 2)*, smoothing it down

1 Coat the reverse side of each fabric image with decoupage medium.

2 When the motif is in place, smooth it down with your hands and fingertips to remove air bubbles or wrinkles.

with your fingers to secure it and to remove air bubbles. Use your fingernail to work the fabric into any grooves or corners. Coat the image and the area surrounding it with decoupage medium *(step 3)*. When the medium dries, apply several coats of sealer.

3 Brush a top coat of decoupage medium over the image, overlapping it onto the immediate surrounding surface.

Stamped and Sponged Finishes

All of the stamping and sponging techniques are easy and fun to do. Rubber stamping and foam shape stamping can be applied to a surface in a random or planned pattern. Stamping can be used to create the effect of wallpaper. Depending on the design of the stamp itself, the results can look traditional, whimsical, or abstract. A fleur-de-lis motif applied in a regularly spaced pattern in gold on a navy blue background has a feeling totally different from multicolored teacups floating haphazardly on a sky-blue background, for example. Likewise, the effect of overall sponging can vary greatly, depending on the colors and the density with which the paint is applied.

STAMPING WITH FOAM SHAPES

YOU WILL NEED: Acrylic paint for the base coat • Acrylic glazes in assorted colors • Precut foam shapes • Flat paintbrushes • Fine artist's paintbrushes ($\frac{1}{2}$-inch flat) • Paper towels • Pencil

Paint the surface with two coats of the base color, and allow it to dry. Using the $\frac{1}{2}$-inch flat artist's brushes, load the foam shapes with colored glazes *(step 1)*. Use

1 Load the stamp with a colored glaze using a flat brush. You can apply one color or two.

2 Apply the wet stamp to the surface. Don't try to make each imprint uniform. It's okay to vary the density of paint and color.

more than one color on each stamp to add dimension. Press the stamp firmly onto the surface *(step 2)*. Overlap and change direction of the markings, and vary the colors, if desired. Reload the stamp with paint for each application. If the image is too light, don't stamp over it. Instead, wipe off the wet paint with a moist paper towel, and then restamp when the area is dry. Keep in mind that a spontaneous approach works best. Don't worry about making each impression perfect. Variations make the look more interesting. Wipe off or wash the stamp before applying a different-color paint.

RUBBER STAMPING

YOU WILL NEED: Acrylic paint for the base coat • Rubber stamps • Raised ink pad • Flat paintbrushes • Paper towels • Pencil • Ruler

Paint the surface or object with two coats of the base color, and allow it to dry. For an evenly spaced-out

1 Load the rubber stamp evenly with ink from an ink pad.

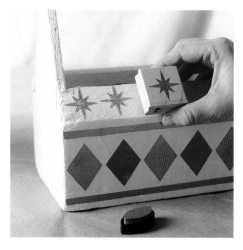

2 Holding the stamp, make a firm impression with it on the surface. Reload it with ink each time you make a new impression.

pattern, you'll have to measure the area, then decide how many passes with the stamp you'll need and how far apart to make each one. Note the position of each stamped image with a pencil, and then load the rubber stamp with ink from the pad *(step 1)*. Press the stamp firmly onto the surface *(step 2)*. Reload with ink before each application. Wash and dry the stamp before switching to a new color. When applying ink to the stamp, be sure to cover the design each time so that you're not left with gaps in the impression.

SPONGING

YOU WILL NEED: Acrylic paint for the base coat, plus three or more additional colors for sponging • Flat foam brushes • Natural sponges • Paper towels • Painter's tape

Paint the object with two coats of the base color, and allow it to dry. Prepare a separate paint palette and sponge for each color. (With small objects, you can reuse a sponge by washing out the paint and wringing out excess moisture.) Experiment with different color combinations. Contrasting hues will produce a stronger look while related tones will have a subtler effect. Mask off areas where you do not want to apply paint. To begin, lightly dip the natural sponge into the first color; then dab it gingerly around the surface of the project *(step 1)*. Change the direction of the sponge often to avoid a repetitious pattern. Apply additional colors, one at a time *(step 2)*. For a more

1 Load the sponge with a light coat of paint, and then gently dab it onto the surface.

2 Apply consecutive colors into areas that reveal only the base-coat color, but do not obscure it completely. To vary texture, use different-size sponges for each color.

open and airy effect, do not apply dense layers of paint, but do feel free to overlap and blend colors.

SPONGING BLOCKS

YOU WILL NEED: Acrylic paint for the base coat, plus assorted additional colors • Flat foam paint-brushes • Fine artist's paintbrushes: flat, liner, pointed, and round in assorted sizes • Cellulose kitchen sponges in desired size • Paper towels • Coated paper plates • Pencil • Ruler or straightedge

Paint the surface with two coats of the base color, and allow it to dry. The painted blocks will be the size of your sponge. If you want to create custom-size blocks for your surface, you can cut the sponges down. You may have to cheat a little if you cannot divide the surface into an even number of blocks. To make this less noticeable, begin your row in the center of the piece, and work toward the outside edges where a smaller end block is less noticeable than if it were to fall dead center. You can create straight rows of blocks or reproduce the stagger of a brick pattern.

Use a separate paper-plate palette and sponge for each color of paint. Wet each sponge with water and wring out the excess moisture. Press the sponge into the paint, and then offload some of the paint onto paper towels to avoid paint drips and runs. Firmly press the sponge onto the surface to make a clear impression *(step 1)*. Do the same thing with each alternating color, leaving about $1/4$ inch of space between each imprint *(step 2)*. Wipe drips with

1 Press a sponge that has been loaded with paint, and blotted, firmly onto the surface.

2 The final effect demonstrates consecutive rows of blocks in alternating colors. Leave a 1/4-inch space between each block.

a damp sponge while the paint is still wet. Reload each sponge with paint and blot it before every application.

The blocks do not have to be perfect. Unevenness in the application of the paint and slightly wobbly edges will simply add charm and texture to the overall effect. Unlike a faux finish that should be as realistic as possible, creating blocks or bricks with a sponge is a technique that is intended to look hand painted.

WHERE TO GO FOR INSPIRATION

Museums and restored historic homes often contain beautiful examples of furniture and accessories that have been decorated with traditional paint techniques. Even if there's a "No Touching Allowed" policy, to actually see the authentic pieces in person is exciting and an education in itself. Remember that most of the antique examples you'll see in such places were painted and decorated with pigments and materials that are no longer available and that time has added a luster and patina newer examples just can't completely reproduce.

Antique and interior-design shops can also provide an instant education. High-end antique stores often feature fine examples of painted furniture that you can study up close. And many of today's design shops carry professionally decorated newer pieces that, while they might seem intimidating to recreate for the novice, can also be immensely inspiring.

Craft shows and boutiques usually feature some contemporary furniture makers that have mastered one or many finishing techniques. Again, the level of expertise might be way beyond what you even aspire to, but it is another good way to see what is in fashion. Sometimes you can get great ideas for using color or combining techniques just by looking at what other people have done.

With the renaissance of painted finishes that is occurring all over the world today, classes and seminars are popping up everywhere. Many classes aren't expensive to attend, either, especially if you are just looking for a basic course to get you started. Check out the course listings at local art schools or at the high schools in your area, or inquire about courses at your neighborhood craft shop.

PART II:
A HOUSE TOUR

It doesn't require an interior designer or a big budget to add character to your home. All it takes is some imagination and a little effort. The most simple painted finishes lend a distinctive texture and visual interest to even the plainest surfaces and most basic shapes. Adding a delicate hand-painted border or a witty decoupage embellishment can elevate mundane objects to one-of-a-kind treasures. By combining several techniques in one project, you can create the look of the expensive accessories available only from high-end catalogs and boutiques. The best news is that you don't need tons of time—most of the projects in this section can be completed over a weekend. Whether you are reviving an old object or enhancing a new one, a decorative finish will add your unique flair to it. As you read through the house tour section of this book, you'll find ideas you may want to copy exactly or adapt for something else you have in mind. Just let your imagination soar, and enjoy the creative process.

The Techniques
DISTRESSING
RUBBING A GOLD FINISH
MARBLING
STENCILING
COLOR WASHING
STAMPING

A Lovely Living Room

"The fireplace must be the focus of every rational scheme of arrangement." —Edith Wharton

The art of topiary provides the theme for the opening chapter of A House Tour. A classic palette of cream and green with accents of antique gold creates an elegant yet down-to-earth feeling. Because the living room is the most public room in the home, it should reflect who you are and evoke a feeling of hospitality. Thus, it's the perfect place to add unique designer accessories, especially if you're the designer.

Every room needs a focal point, something that provides a visual anchor. Here a fabulous fireplace screen does the trick. You can construct a simple screen out of plywood to fit your specifications. If you don't have a fireplace to work with, you can translate this design into a room-dividing screen or adapt it for a flat-panel door to create a dramatic entrance. Decorating the screen takes some advance planning and involves several techniques—stamping, color washing, and stenciling—but it can easily be completed in two weekends.

Wonderful tables are essential living room accessories, and the look of stone adds a sense of solidity while introducing interesting texture. A classic faux-marble tabletop complements virtually any style decor. The marbling technique is deceptively easy to do and would be appropriate on any smooth surface, from coffee table to dresser top. A few coats of glossy sealer gives it a lustrous sheen and protects it against use. If you've chosen a different palette for your room than the one shown here, you may want to look for a marble sample that coordinates with your color scheme and use that to copy for your project.

The planter dressed up with paint and a metallic stenciled-and-stamped design is actually an old chicken feeder, spotted outside an antique store. What a stroke of luck that it fit perfectly on the mantel shelf! An unfinished lamp base with simple trim begs for a repeat of the topiary theme. Fabric and a touch of fringe add pretty details to the shade.

End Table

You Will Need

- Unfinished wood table
- Primer
- Satin finish latex paint in off-white
- Acrylic craft paints in French Vanilla, Wicker White, Dapple Gray, and Caramel
- Decorator glazes in Tuscan Russet and Russet Brown
- Paint extender
- Paint thickener
- Metallic wax finish in Gold Classic
- Denatured alcohol
- Stippling brush
- Spatter brush
- Goose point feather
- Candle wax
- Antiquing wax or brown shoe polish
- Sandpaper and tack cloth
- Steel wool
- Multipurpose primer
- Flat foam paintbrushes
- Fine artist's paintbrushes, medium round
- Sponges, natural
- Masking tape
- Craft knife
- Mixing containers
- Paper towels
- Paper
- Soft lint-free cloths
- Pencil and scissors
- Ruler or straightedge
- Glossy sealer

How do you define traditional style today? The look is far less conservative and more eclectic than in the past. It still includes any of the classic elements typically associated with eighteenth- and nineteenth-century design—carved panels and trim, polished brass and silver, rich carpets, fabrics, and patterns—but its updated appearance is less ornamented. While it transcends fads, the new look embraces fresh ideas, too.

Directions

Sand the table to create a smooth surface, wipe clean with a tack cloth, then apply one coat of primer. Let it dry. Following the directions for Distressing (page 33), rub the edges of the table legs and drawer knobs with candle wax, which will help simulate the uneven texture of age. Cover the table base with one coat of off-white paint. Allow it to dry, and then sand over the waxed areas to remove most of the paint. Rub antiquing wax or shoe polish over the surface. Following the directions for Rubbing a Gold Finish (page 47), massage gold wax over the knobs and edges of the table to add highlights. Paint the tabletop with two or more coats of French Vanilla paint. Let it dry. Following the directions for Marbling (page 42), create a faux-marble finish on the tabletop. To mimic the look of polished stone, apply two coats of a high-gloss sealer.

You Will Need

- Wooden feedbox
- Primer
- Satin finish latex paint in off-white
- Metallic acrylic craft paint in Gold and Solid Bronze
- Stencil
- Metallic gold wax
- Rubber stamp
- Gold raised ink stamp pad
- Stencil brushes
- Spray adhesive
- Sandpaper and tack cloth
- Steel wool
- Heavy-duty primer
- Flat foam paintbrushes
- Masking or painter's tape
- Craft knife
- Paper towels
- Soft lint-free cloths
- Pencil
- Ruler or straightedge
- Sealer

Mantel Planter

Directions

Sand the box, and then wipe it clean with a tack cloth. Apply one or two coats of primer as needed. Let it dry. Paint the box with two coats of off-white paint. When the box is dry, arrange a diamond-and-line border stencil on its front and side panels, and mark the placement. Following the directions for Positive Stenciling (page 39) and referring to the photo, above right, for placement, stencil every other diamond and all of the line borders with Gold paint. Wait for the paint to dry before stenciling the remaining diamonds with Solid Bronze paint. Make note of a place in the center along the top edge of the front panel and on the sides of the planter for the star design. Following the directions for Rubber Stamping (page 51), apply gold stars. Following the directions for Rubbing a Gold Finish (page 47), rub gold wax along the edges of the box. Finish it with two coats of sealer.

What are traditional-style details? Rich woods and finishes, such as maple, mahogany, and mellow oak, enhance the look, as do opulent upholstery and drapery fabrics. Embellish them with *passementerie:* decorative trims, tassels, fringe, woven bands, rosettes, and cords. Accent a traditional-style room with a touch of glitz in the form of gilding or rich marble.

Fireplace Screen

You Will Need

- Wooden fireplace screen
- Primer
- Decorative base molding
- Satin finish latex paint in off-white
- Metallic acrylic craft paint in Gold and Antique Gold
- Decorator glazes in neutral, Italian Sage, Russet Brown, Sage Green, Ivy Green, Deep Woods Green, and Patina
- Stencils
- Sponge stamp block in ivy shape
- Scroll stamp
- Antiquing medium in Apple Butter Brown
- Liquid leaf in Classic Gold
- 3-inch flat-bristle paintbrush
- Stencil brushes
- Waxed stencil paper
- Kraft paper
- Sandpaper and tack cloth
- Primer
- Flat foam paint-brushes
- Fine artist's paint-brushes: flat, liner, pointed, and round in assorted sizes
- Masking tape
- Craft knife, scissors
- Mixing containers
- Paper towels
- Pencil
- Straightedge
- Sealer

What architectural features are typical of traditional style?
Look for elements of fine craftsmanship: wood flooring; trim with fluted or carved panels and corner blocks; decorative crown and base moldings; paneled doors; muntined windows; wood railings with turned balusters and elegant newel posts; mantels and fireplace jambs decorated with composition ornament or carved details; ceiling medallions; columns; brackets; cornices; and wainscoting.

Directions

You'll need a hinged three-panel wooden fireplace screen, which you can buy or make. If you buy one, you'll have to sand and prime it thoroughly before applying the new finish over the existing one. Ideally, it's best to work on unfinished wood. The screen used for this project features two 9- x 36-inch side panels and one 26- x 36-inch center panel that were cut from a ¾-inch-thick sheet of plywood. If you aren't handy with a circular saw or table saw, ask your local lumber mill to cut the panels to your desired dimensions. Attach the side and center panels with two-way (piano) hinges, which are easy to install. Simply mark their location along the inside edges of the panel pieces, drill pilot holes, and then screw them into place.

Remove the hinges, and set them aside. Lightly sand the panels, and then wipe them clean with a tack cloth. Cut strips of 2-inch decorative base molding to fit the width of the panels, and glue the pieces along the bottom of each section. After the glue sets, apply two coats of primer to the panels. Let the primer dry, and then paint the panels with two coats of off-white latex paint.

Cut stencils for the topiary, roping, and lattice (pages 64, 66, 67), following directions for Making Your Own Stencil (page 40).

Using a straightedge, draw a $3^1/2$-inch-wide border along the top and both sides of the center panel, and along the tops and outer sides of the other two panels. Just below this border, measure and draw a $^1/2$-inch-wide band at the top of the center panel and along the sides, top, and bottom of the other panels.

Arrange and mark the position of the topiary, roping, and lattice stencils on the panels. (You'll have to repeat the lattice down the length of each side panel.) Remove the stencil templates until later.

Mask the $3^1/2$-inch border and $^1/2$-inch band; then paint the middle section of each panel with the Apple Butter Brown antiquing medium. While the finish is still wet, rub some off with a soft cloth to make it look as though it has become slightly worn over time. After the medium dries, remove the masking tape.

Mix the Italian Sage and neutral glaze to your desired shade. Mask the inside and outside edges of the $3^1/2$-inch border. Following directions for Color Washing (page 30), apply the glaze inside the border on all panels, making crosshatched strokes with a 3-inch-wide flat brush. Let the glaze dry, and then remove the tape.

Mask the inside and outside edges of the $^1/2$-inch band, then fill it in with the Antique Gold using a $^1/2$-inch-wide flat brush. Let it dry, then remove the tape.

Measure and mark the placement of the border's stamped scroll motif. Following directions for Rubber Stamping (page 51), load the stamp with Antique Gold paint using a flat brush, and apply the design.

Following directions for Stenciling (page 39), place the template into position on the panel, and apply the twisted rope pattern along the sides and bottom of the middle section of the center panel using the Antique Gold paint. Remove the template. Follow the same procedure and stencil the lattice onto the side panels.

Stencil the large pot (page 65) in Gold, adding shading with an artist's brush and the Russet Brown. (For the pot shown in the photo, see the Sources on page 126.) For the topiary, mix a tiny amount of green with the neutral glaze and paint one 5-inch and one $7^1/2$-inch round form (paint the smaller one above the other). Stencil the stem in Russet Brown. With the ivy sponge stamp, fill in with leaves, overlapping and varying direction, using the three green glazes. Add veining with a fine artist's brush.

Highlight molding with the liquid leaf, apply two coats of sealer, and then reinstall the hinges.

Table Lamp

You Will Need

- Unfinished wooden lamp base
- Self-adhesive lampshade, 8x14x11 inches
- Fabric with topiary print
- 1¼ yards of fringe trim in a shade to match the fabric
- ¾ yard of flat braid trim in a shade to match the fabric
- Hot-glue gun and glue sticks
- Metallic acrylic craft paint in French Vanilla, Antique Gold and Old Ivy
- Decorator glaze in Russet Brown, Italian Sage, Deep Woods Green, and Patina
- Rubber eraser
- Lattice stencil
- Antiquing medium in Brown
- Liquid leaf in Classic Gold
- Stencil blanks or paper
- Stencil brushes
- Transfer paper
- Spray adhesive
- Sandpaper and tack cloth
- Steel wool
- Multipurpose primer
- Flat foam paintbrushes
- Masking tape
- Craft knife
- Paper towels
- Soft lint-free cloths
- Pencil
- Ruler or straightedge
- Scissors

What
is traditional-style furniture?

Classic American and English designs, such as Chippendale, Hepplewhite, and Queen Anne, fall into this style category. A handsome wing chair, a camelback sofa and a table or side chair with cabriole legs are mainstays. Don't be afraid to mix different pieces, but include a unifying element, usually the color scheme, to tie them together.

Directions

Sand the lamp base to create a smooth surface. Wipe it with a tack cloth, and then apply two coats of the primer. Paint the two sides, flat bottom, and top of the base with two coats of Old Ivy paint. Let the paint dry.

Mask the edges of the green areas, and then paint the front and back panels with two coats of French Vanilla paint. When it dries, apply a coat of antiquing medium to the front and back panels. While the medium is still wet, rub some off in an uneven manner with a soft cloth. Remove the masking tape.

On a photocopier, resize the topiary and lattice stencils to a size suitable for your lamp base, or following the directions for Making Your Own Stencil (page 40), create new templates. Following the directions for Stenciling (page 39), create the topiary for the front panel, beginning with the

Directions *continued*

container, which is applied with the Antique Gold paint, then the stem, using the Russet Brown glaze.

For the round topiary forms, use a pale mixture of the green and neutral glazes applied with an artist's brush. Paint one above the other, making the top form smaller than the other, as shown in the photo.

While they are drying, make your stamp for the ivy leaves. With a craft knife, cut a small leaf shape into an ordinary rubber pencil eraser. Following the directions for Rubber Stamping (page 51), load and off-load the carved eraser with the various green glazes and randomly fill in the topiary balls with leaves. Overlap and change direction for a realistic look of intertwined ivy. Repeat the design on the back panel.

Stencil the lattice on each of the green-painted side panels in Antique Gold. Following the directions for Rubbing a Gold Finish (page 47), rub gold wax along the edges of the lamp's base. In this case, the base is attached to four wooden balls, which have been painted with liquid gold leaf. Finish the lamp base with two or more coats of sealer.

Remove the protective paper from the self-adhesive lampshade. Using the paper as a pattern, cut the topiary fabric to the same dimensions. Following the manufacturer's instructions, smooth the fabric in place on the lampshade. Cut a length of flat braid to fit around the lampshade's top edge, overlapping the ends. Using the hot-glue gun, glue the flat braid in place. Cut a length of fringe trim to fit along the lower edge of the lampshade. Glue the fringe in place.

ALTERNATIVE SOFT TRIMMINGS FOR YOUR SHADE

Flat Gimp: You'll recognize this as the trim that covers upholstery tacks on your furniture, but you can apply this woven band, which comes in sizes up to $^1/_2$ inch wide, to anything.

Tassel Fringe: This looped fringe with tassels can be used on curtains, cushions, pillows, or table skirts, but it can add visual interest to a lampshade as well.

Rope: As the name implies, this is a cord of braided fabric. You can find rope in various sizes, but make sure the type you select is in keeping with the scale of your project.

Fringe: The type pictured is actually called Bullion Fringe. It features plain or twisted cords that fall like a skirt from a band. Fringe is available in numerous lengths.

Patterns

Follow the directions for Making Your Own Stencil (page 40) using these patterns as a guide. Enlarge or reduce these images on a copier to make them the correct scale for your project. To purchase ready-made stencils, see the Sources on page 126.

STEM

TOPIARY GLOBES

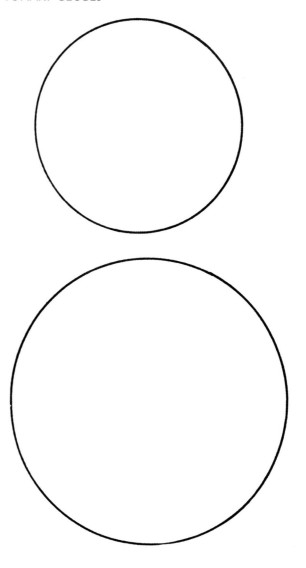

SMALL POT

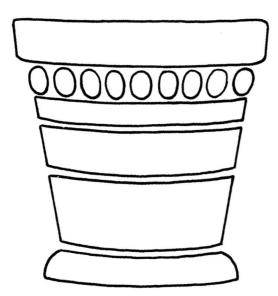

LARGE POT

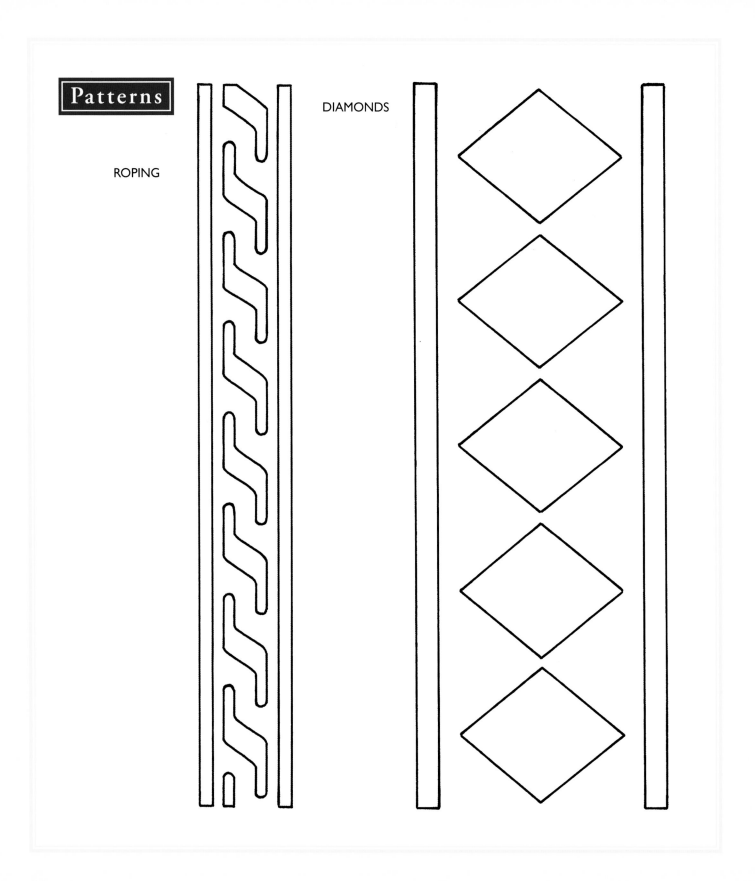

Patterns

ROPING

DIAMONDS

LATTICE

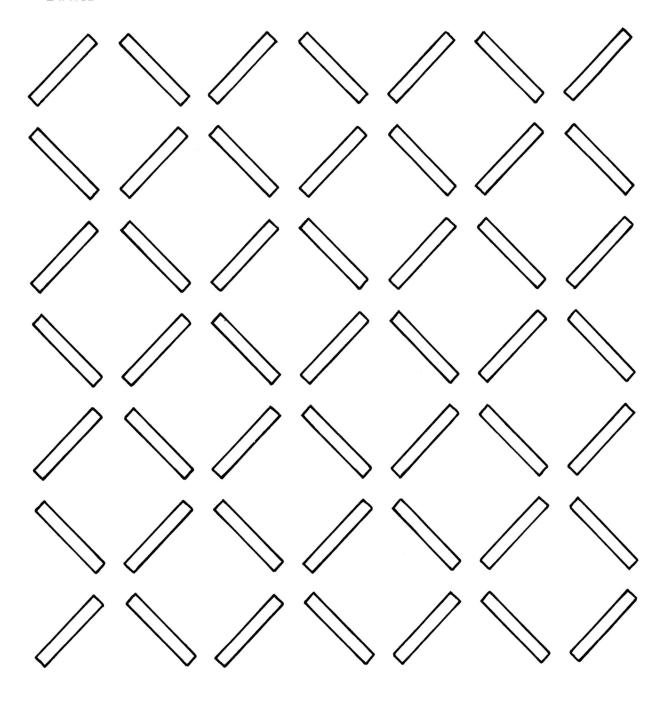

The Techniques
GOLD LEAFING
SPONGING
PAPER DECOUPAGE
HAND PAINTING
RUBBING A GOLD FINISH

A Bedroom to Dream In

"And I will make thee beds of roses . . ."—Christopher Marlowe

Abedroom at its best should be a retreat from the stresses of the world—an oasis of comfort. A charming faded floral cottage-print wallcovering and fabric helped to create this example and became the point of departure for a romantic flower-filled bedroom. With this important ingredient in place, it was easy to pull together the coordinating elements.

A headboard can be new or a discovery at a flea market or garage sale—the one pictured here was found in a junk shop. If your find has been finished in a dark stain, avoid the mess of stripping it; instead, sand it down, and then prime it with a heavy-duty, all-purpose primer. Apply several coats of the mellow green base color, and create texture with a simple tri-color sponging technique. It might be tedious cutting out the rather intricate floral motifs from wallpaper, but with sharp scissors and patience, it's well worth the effort. A charming hand-painted vine and gold accents highlight the floral design and add to the cottage charm of the piece.

A side chair such as the one shown here (another thrift-store find) can be easily transformed with paint, simple gilded accents, and a seat upholstered in coordinating fabric. You might not find an exact replica of this chair, but use these techniques to embellish whatever style chair you discover—preferably one that has a center panel on the back and a padded seat.

A wicker-and-wood tray with a glass insert, embellished with old cards and fabric, is ideal for breakfast in bed. When you spot one at a yard sale, grab it.

The stripes-and-vine three-drawer dresser involves a bit of planning ahead and some simple hand painting. If you can, use an unfinished piece because it provides a clean surface for the painting. Plan the hand painting carefully, and mark the position of the flowers and connecting vines with a chalk pencil, which can be wiped off later.

The tin pitcher is easy to paint—just pick an accent color from the wallpaper, add ornamentation with a single rose motif, and accent with gold.

Side Chair

You Will Need

- Wooden side chair
- Latex satin paint in off-white
- Acrylic craft paint in Poetry Green and Aspen Green
- Artist's pigments in light red oxide
- Green floral fabric
- Batting
- Staple gun
- Sheets of imitation gold leaf
- Gold leaf adhesive
- Antiquing wax or

- brown shoe polish
- Soft natural-bristle paintbrush
- Talcum powder
- Sandpaper
- Steel wool
- Heavy-duty primer
- Flat foam paintbrushes
- Soft lint-free cloths
- Mixing containers
- Chalk pencil
- Ruler or straightedge
- Scissors
- Sealer

What is cottage style? This look recalls Grandmother's house or a home at the beach. It's nostalgic, comforting, and relaxed, and says "leave your troubles behind." To create the cottage style, layer fabrics, preferably faded florals, ticking stripes, chenille, and vintage linens with touches of needlepoint and quilts. Accent with an odd piece or two of furniture from the 1940s.

Directions

Remove the padded seat from the chair. Sand the wood to create a smooth surface, and then paint it with two coats of primer. While it dries, mix the Poetry Green and Aspen Green paints to create a shade that matches the background of the floral fabric. Paint the center back strut or panel with two coats of the mixed green.

Cover the center of the back rung with red oxide paint; then following the directions for Gold Leafing (page 46), accent selected areas. Paint the remainder of the chair with two coats of off-white latex satin paint.

When it's dry, go over it lightly with steel wool and rub antiquing wax or shoe polish into the gold leafing for a slightly worn look. Apply two coats of sealer.

To recover the chair seat, use the old one as a pattern, cutting several pieces of batting and one piece of fabric to the same dimensions plus 3 inches all around. Position batting on the top side of the seat, fold the excess underneath, staple it in place, and trim away excess. Cover the batting with fabric, folding and stapling the excess to the underside. Attach the refurbished cushion.

You Will Need

- Wooden headboard
- Latex satin paint in green
- Acrylic craft paint in Cappuccino, Poetry Green, Green Meadow, and Taffy
- Floral wallpaper
- Decoupage medium
- Metallic wax finish in Renaissance
- Sandpaper
- Steel wool
- Tack cloth
- Heavy-duty primer
- Flat paintbrushes:

- foam or bristle
- Fine artist's paintbrushes: #4 liner, medium pointed
- One natural sponge for each color paint
- Chalk pencil
- Painter's tape
- Craft knife
- Paper towels
- Soft lint-free cloths
- Pencil
- Ruler or straightedge
- Sharp-pointed scissors
- Sealer

Floral Headboard

Directions

*S*and the headboard to a smooth surface, and then apply two coats of heavy-duty primer. Let the primer dry; then apply two coats of the satin green base.

Mask the frame of the headboard. Following the directions for Sponging (page 51), sponge-paint the center panel with Taffy, Cappuccino, and Poetry Green paint.

Cut out three large and two small floral motifs from the wallpaper. Once the paint has dried, you can arrange the paper flowers inside the center panel, as shown above right. Mark their placement with the chalk pencil. Following the directions for Paper Decoupage (page 48), apply the floral motifs. Let them dry. Remove the masking tape from the frame of the headboard, and

then carefully mask the center panel of the headboard.

Draw a wavy line with chalk pencil down the center of the frame pieces for the ivy vine placement. Following directions for Simple Hand Painting (page 37), use the Green Meadow acrylic paint and the pointed brush to create small leaves that appear to be coming from either side of the wavy line. Using the liner brush, paint over the chalk line to connect the leaves.

Following the directions for Rubbing a Gold Finish (page 47), embellish the edges of the frame and posts. Remove the tape. Finish with two coats of sealer.

Serving Tray

Directions

Remove the tray back and glass panel. If necessary, sand the wood to create a smooth surface; then wipe it with a tack cloth.

Following the manufacturer's instructions and holding the can 2 to 4 feet from the project, spray-paint a fine mist of Soft Green paint onto the tray to cover it completely. Move the spray can back and forth to cover evenly and thoroughly. Work in a well-ventilated area. Cover the tray with two coats of paint, taking care to get inside the grooves and crevices of the tray. Spraying large amounts of paint in crevices will result in drips, so it's best to build up several layers of a fine mist.

Using the tray back as a pattern, cut a piece of fabric, adding $^1/_2$ inch all around. Spray the back side of the fabric with the adhesive. With the right side facing up, smooth the fabric over the tray back. Turn the raw edges over to the underside of the tray back, and miter the corners of the fabric. Arrange the postcards and photographs over the fabric as you desire. Spray the reverse side of each piece with adhesive. Mount and smooth the pieces in place. Clean the glass to remove dirt and finger marks; then reinsert it into the tray.

How do you decorate with cottage-style accessories? Display collections of your favorite things: old family photos in fun frames, cushy pillows, souvenirs. Tables draped with vintage dresser scarves make perfect settings for collectible knickknacks or vases. Decorate a wall with pretty plates, slightly tattered prints, antique purses, and straw hats. Sort through those boxes and trunks of miscellany that you've had squirreled away for years. You'll find treasures you forgot you had.

You Will Need

- Galvanized tin pitcher
- Acrylic gloss enamel paint in Eggshell and Beachcomber Beige
- Metallic acrylic paint in Solid Bronze
- Oval stencil template
- Decoupage medium
- Metallic wax finish in Copper
- Rose wallpaper
- Steel wool
- Tack cloth
- Metal primer spray paint
- Flat foam paintbrushes
- Fine artist's paintbrushes: liner, pointed and small round in assorted sizes
- Spray adhesive
- Paper towels
- Soft lint-free cloths
- Chalk pencil
- Ruler or straightedge
- Sharp-pointed scissors
- Sealer

Tin Pitcher

Directions

Following the manufacturer's instructions and holding the can 2 to 4 feet from the project, spray-paint a fine mist of primer at the pitcher to coat it completely. Move the spray can back and forth to cover the surface evenly and thoroughly. Work in a well-ventilated space. Apply two coats of primer, getting it into the grooves and crevices of the pitcher. Spraying large amounts of the primer in crevices will result in drips, so it's better to build up several thin coats of paint.

When the pitcher is dry, paint it with two coats of Beachcomer Beige using the flat foam brush.

Following the directions for Simple Hand Painting (page 37), trace a large oval on one side of the pitcher, and fill it in with the Eggshell paint. Cut a small rose motif from the wallpaper. Following the directions for Paper Decoupage (page 48), apply the rose to the center of the oval.

Using the chalk pencil, draw a line around the oval to use as a guide for a leaf border. With the bronze acrylic paint and the round paint brushes, create a border line. Make small leaves on either side of the border. Following the directions for Rubbing a Gold Finish (page 47), rub the copper wax along the edges of the pitcher. When all is dry, finish the pitcher with two coats of protective sealer.

Striped Dresser

You Will Need

- *Three-drawer unfinished wood dresser*
- *Latex satin paint in cream and green*
- *Acrylic craft paint in Portrait Light, Naphthol Green, Poetry Green, Mystic Green, Old Ivy, and Burgundy*
- *Sandpaper and tack cloth*
- *Steel wool*
- *Multipurpose primer*
- *Flat foam paintbrushes*
- *Fine artist's paintbrushes: flat, liner, pointed, and round in assorted sizes*
- *Masking or painter's tape*
- *Craft knife*
- *Paper towels*
- *Chalk pencil*
- *Ruler or straightedge*
- *Sealer*

What
fabrics do you use with
the cottage style? Try combining
fabrics like faded florals, ticking stripes,
and vintage linens and layering them in a
loose, relaxed way. Slipcovers, the more wrinkled
and faded the better, add to the comfy appeal. Pile
cushy pillows on couches, chairs, and beds. Even if
vintage fabrics aren't in mint condition, they can
be used to fashion fabulous pillows. Look
for chenille bedspreads, lace curtains,
tattered quilts, and lovely bits of
needlepoint.

Directions

Remove all drawers and hardware from the dresser. Sand the dresser and drawers to create a smooth surface. Wipe them clean with a tack cloth, and then apply two coats of the primer.

To create the stripes, replace the drawers, and then divide the top and front of the dresser into an odd number of vertical panels. Mark them with a straightedge and a chalk pencil. Each stripe in the example pictured here is approximately 4 inches wide, but yours may be wider or narrower, depending on the overall width of your piece. In the same manner, mark out stripes along the sides of the dresser.

Remove the drawers to make painting easier. Beginning with the center stripe, run a line of masking tape along the outside edges of every other stripe. Smooth down and burnish the edges of the tape with your fingers to secure it in place.

Using a wide foam brush, paint the center and every alternate stripe with two or more coats of the green satin latex paint. Allow it to dry. Remove the tape, and then mask the alternate stripes in the same manner with new tape. Paint these stripes with a clean foam brush using two or more coats of the cream paint. Let it dry. Remove the masking tape.

To create the trellis design on the front, divide the drawer panels into three sections. The center section should consist of three stripes, with two stripes comprising the sections to the left and right of the center. With a chalk pencil and a straightedge, make a straight line along the outside edges of each center section. Within each section, draw a line from each corner to the opposite one; then make a small "+" in middle of each section. You'll use all of these lines as guides. Thin the

Poetry Green paint with a small amount of water. Following directions for Simple Hand Painting (page 37), create tiny leaves along the first lines that you drew using the pointed brush. Then paint wavy lines along each "X" with a liner brush. Arrange the leaves staggered or emanating in a straight line as you desire. Using a round brush, make small Burgundy rosebuds or bouquets in the center of the "+." Use all the colors in your palette for the flowers and double- or triple-load your paintbrush to add dimension and shades. Add the leaves at all four points of the "+." Divide the top and sides of the dresser in half lengthwise to paint their trellis patterns. Make a large flower arrangement in the center of the dresser top. When your hand painting dries, apply two or more coats of sealer to the entire piece. When that dries, replace the old hardware, and insert the drawers.

TIPS ON PAINTING STRIPES

Stripes are among the most attractive painted effects you can add to a surface. Broad, even stripes, such as the ones used on the dresser featured in this chapter, can go on fairly quickly and evenly. If your hand isn't particularly steady, you may want to roll on the paint rather than use a brush to apply it. You can find narrow rollers in paint and craft shops, or you can cut down a standard-size roller to the desired width of the stripe. It's best to use a thick paint with this application as opposed to a thin glaze because you have to make one uninterrupted pass with the roller. Avoid running the roller up and down.

Load the roller from a paint tray. Start at the top, and run the roller straight down (or across) the surface. For a neat look, mask the edges before applying the paint.

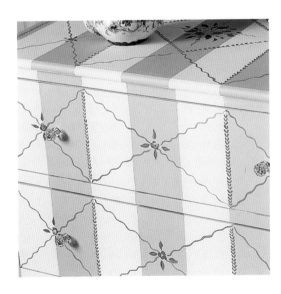

A Gentleman's Study

"No man but feels more of a man in the world if he have a bit of ground to call his own."—Charles Dudley Weaver

In presenting a well-rounded decorating scheme, here's a group of projects with a clearly masculine look. Bolder techniques and colors work well for the accouterments in a man's study. In this case, traditional desk accessories in simple but strong finishes coordinate with the rich dark wood of an antique desk. A quick trip to an office-supply store will provide most of the items you'll need to get started. By the time you're done, the room will look as if you've outfitted it with things from an exclusive stationer.

It was easy to transform a plain leather letter caddy in minutes using a fleur-de-lis stamp and some gold wax. The burgundy-color leather perfectly complements the antique book jackets, too.

The addition of several unique art papers easily turned a standard-issue desk pad into a custom accessory, as well. Rich colors and textures of handmade papers always add a sense of luxury.

For a tired-looking carved cedar box that cried for creative refinishing, an inlay effect using a combination of malachite and rubbed-gold finishes worked like magic. The result is so handsome, the box could make a wonderful, personal gift for a writer, an executive, or a graduate.

A chunky pair of plaster bookends purchased at a crafts-supply store became objets d'art in under an hour with the help of some basic gilding supplies and skills. If you can't find suitable bookends, buy an inexpensive bust to create a stylish desktop accessory. Thanks to modern materials, gilding is now both easy and affordable to do. And any imperfections simply add to the aged effect.

Good lighting is a desk-area essential, but interesting lamps are hard to come by and tend to be costly. Adding a patina finish to an ordinary second-hand one gives it a sophisticated ambiance and highlights the marble base of the lamp in the example. For the finishing touch, wrap a plain shade in tissue paper with an antique map motif.

Desk Caddy

You Will Need

- Leather desk caddy
- Raised-surface stamp and pad with gold ink
- Fleur-de-lis stamp, 1¼ inches
- Metallic wax finish
- in Renaissance Gold
- Paper towels
- Soft lint-free cloths
- Pencil
- Ruler or straightedge
- Scissors

Directions

Clean the caddy with a soft cloth; use leather cleaner if necessary.

Following the directions for Rubber Stamping (page 51), mark the placement of the design all around the caddy to create one or more rows or bands. In this case, the design is a fleur-de-lis (page 83), a popular and classic heraldic motif, but you can select any raised-stamp design for your project. Once you've mapped out where you want the image to appear, load the stamp with gold ink, and then apply it. The stamp should be evenly covered, but not dripping with ink. Reload as needed. To replicate the gold border around the top and bottom of the caddy, follow the directions for Stenciling (page 39). You can make a template for the stencil using the pattern on page 83. If desired, rub the edges with gold wax, following the directions for Rubbing a Gold Finish (page 47).

How do you define "masculine" style? The look of an Edwardian smoking room comes to mind, with a large antique desk, a humidor, maps, handsome bound books, and leather upholstery, but a sturdy wooden table with a drawer and a good-looking desk set makes a practical alternative. While old wooden file cabinets are costly and difficult to come by, older metal ones have that 1930s Humphrey Bogart romance about them and can be easily painted to fit with your color scheme. Inexpensive bookshelves, too, can be transformed with paint and, when filled with a combination of books, papers, and interesting accessories, can serve the dual purpose of storage and display.

Desk Pad

You Will Need

- Desk blotter
- Green marbled paper
- Textured heavy-weight brown paper
- Decoupage medium
- Spray adhesive
- Flat foam paint-brushes
- Craft knife
- Pencil
- Ruler or straightedge
- Sharp-pointed scissors

Directions

You'll need a plain desk blotter for this project. Because you'll be re-covering the side pockets, you don't have to purchase an expensive leather one, or you may use an old one.

First, measure the width and length of the side pockets. Using a pencil and a straightedge as a guide, draw the shapes to size on the marbled kraft paper, and then cut them out with a craft knife.

Following the directions for Paper Decoupage (page 48), adhere the cut-out paper pieces to the top surface of each side pocket of the desk blotter.

You can buy new blotter paper or fashion one yourself using heavy-duty brown paper. To make your own, remove the old one and measure it. If it's missing, measure the section that the pad normally covers, and add 1 inch to each side to allow for tucking into the side pockets. Cut out a piece of the brown paper to size using a craft knife.

How can you create a study in any size home? It's easier than you might think. Even if you don't have an entire room to devote to a study, you can transform a seldom-trafficked upstairs hallway or even a quiet corner of a room into a home office. The important thing is to find a spot that offers privacy and quiet at the time of day it will be most used. Make it comfortable with at least one upholstered piece, a desk, and a good lamp for reading.

Malachite Box

How should you accessorize a man's study? Make the room as personal as possible. Objects or themes that relate to an individual's interests and hobbies are excellent choices. For someone who likes to travel or sail, group framed maps or seascapes on the walls. If he is a sportsman, perhaps fabric or wallpaper with a golf or fishing theme would be appropriate. Use objects with a strong sense of scale—architectural elements, such as an old mantel or pediment.

Directions

Sand the box to create a smooth surface, and then wipe it with a tack cloth. The box pictured above has a raised-relief pattern. If your box is made of smooth wood, limit the faux-malachite look to the top of the lid. Apply one or more coats of the primer to the entire surface, covering the lid and all four sides. When the primer dries, mask the four sides of the box.

Cover the lid with at least two coats of Pale Green paint. Let it dry. Then coat it with the Dark Green glaze, and following the directions for Malachite (page 41), work the technique over the area. Allow the Malachite to dry, and then mask it. Unmask the four sides of the box; then coat them with Brick Red paint. Apply the Dark Green glaze to the edges of the lid. Following the directions for Rubbing a Gold Finish (page 47), rub gold wax over the relief-patterned edges. Remove masking tape from the Malachite. Finish the box with two or more coats of sealer.

Golden Bookends

You Will Need

- Plaster bookends
- Acrylic craft paint in Brick Red
- Sheets of imitation gold leaf
- Gold leaf adhesive
- Antiquing wax or brown shoe polish
- Soft natural-bristle paintbrush
- Talcum powder
- Multipurpose or heavy-duty primer
- Flat paintbrushes: natural bristle
- Soft lint-free cloths

What
patterns and colors
look best with this style?

Rich hues—burgundy, brown, and deep green—accented with antique gold create a sophisticated, mature ambiance. Paisleys, suiting wools, and tartan plaids are all traditionally masculine-inspired fabrics that are at their best in mix-and-match combinations. Use them for upholstery or curtains, or introduce them with accent pillows or as throws. Anything uphol-stered in leather also adds opulence and comfort to the room. In general, materials with a textured fin-ish will look—and feel—at home here. Pairing them with wood paneling or wood blinds makes a pleasing combination. And don't forget gentle-manly fashion underfoot: Besides adding comfort, a plush Oriental carpet atop a wood floor will pull the entire look together. Take more color cues from its design.

Directions

Wipe off the bookends to remove surface dust or grime, and then prepare them for refinishing with one or more coats of primer. If their surface is less than perfect, all the better for a vintage appearance. Let the primer dry before applying two or more coats of Brick Red paint. Allow the paint to dry.

Following the directions for Gold Leafing (page 46), add gilding to the bookends. (You don't need a uniform finish.) Rub them with antiquing wax or shoe polish, and then apply two coats of sealer.

Desk Lamp

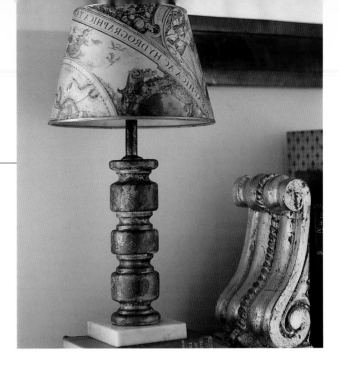

You Will Need

- Wooden lamp base
- Paper lampshade
- Acrylic craft paint in Patina and Old Ivy
- Metallic acrylic craft paint in Antique Copper and Solid Bronze
- Tissue wrapping paper in Old World map print
- Metallic wax finish in Classic Gold
- Spray adhesive
- Large sheet of paper
- Sandpaper and tack cloth
- Multipurpose or heavy-duty primer
- Flat paintbrushes, foam or bristle
- Fine artist's paintbrush, medium round
- Natural sponge
- Masking or painter's tape
- Craft knife
- Paper towels
- Kraft paper
- Soft lint-free cloths
- Pencil
- Ruler or straightedge
- Scissors
- Spray sealer

Directions

Sand the lamp base to create a smooth surface. Wipe it clean with a tack cloth. If the base is turned, carefully clean out any grime that may have accumulated in grooves or twists in the wood. Cover any areas not to be painted with masking tape.

Apply one or more coats of primer. Let it dry. Following the directions for Patina Finishing (page 44), coat the base until you have achieved the desired patina effect. Allow the finish to dry. Following the directions for Rubbing a Gold Finish (page 47), highlight some areas with the gold wax.

Make a pattern for the lampshade cover this way: Place the shade on a large sheet of kraft paper, and then roll it, tracing the top and bottom edges as you go along. Continue rolling and tracing until you've completed the diameter of both the top and bottom of the shade. The result is a flat curved pattern you can cut out and use as a template. Fit it around the lampshade, secure it with a paper clip, and then make any necessary adjustments, such as trimming away excess paper.

Using this paper pattern, cut a piece of decorative tissue paper to the same dimensions. Spray the back side of the tissue paper with spray adhesive, and then place it onto the shade, smoothing as you go. If desired, glue fabric trim along the edges, or rub in gold wax.

Finally, spray both the lampshade and the lamp base with two or more protective coats of sealer.

As an alternative to applying a stamp for the fleur-de-lis pattern on the desk caddy, you can use a stencil. Buy a ready-cut stencil or create your own following the instructions for Making Your Own Stencil (page 40) and using the pattern below. An alternative motif for your desk caddy could be a diamond design. Use the pattern on this page as a guideline for creating a diamond stencil. At the bottom of the page is a template for the caddy's border.

FLEUR-DE-LIS

DIAMOND

BORDER

The Techniques
PAPER DECOUPAGE
RUBBING A GOLD FINISH
GRANITE
RUBBER STAMPING

A Victorian Dressing Room

"Perhaps no other decorative symbol is so associated with the arts of the Victorian period as the acanthus leaf."—The Illustrated Encyclopedia of Victoriana

The richness of a fabric embellished with lush green acanthus leaves on a burgundy background set the tone for a refined Victorian-inspired dressing room. What woman wouldn't enjoy the luxury of a skirted dressing table, coordinating full-length mirror, folding screen, and matching storage boxes?

You might be lucky enough to find an old dressing table set in a thrift shop, but if you don't, a side table and a pretty chair will work just as well. The handsome faux-granite top that was applied to this one pulls out the green tones from the fabric. Protected with a glossy sealer, it provides an attractive surface for displaying elegant grooming accessories. Once the top is finished, it's easy to attach the skirt with decorative upholstery tacks. Paint, rubbed gold accents, and a re-covered seat pad with coordinating trim rejuvenate the old stool.

Victorian folks were mad for decorating storage containers (boxes, trunks) with beautiful cut-out papers. You can adorn a large bandbox with wallpaper that matches the acanthus fabric and add gold foil trim. For an authentic Victorian decoupage effect, use reproduction cutouts to cover a second box. Decorate the smallest box with a delicate flower motif, and trim it with a gold foil band.

Every Victorian household, it seems, appreciated the value of mirrors. Essential to any boudoir was a cheval mirror—a hinged mirror on a stand. You can transform an unfinished pine cheval mirror by staining the frame in a rich rose tone, then stamping it with a leaf design in gold that complements the acanthus leaves on the fabric.

A folding screen was *de rigueur* in a Victorian dressing room. Metallic wax emphasizes raised detailing in the wicker screen used for this project.

Storage Boxes

You Will Need

- Papier-mâché stacking boxes in 3 sizes
- Acrylic craft paint in Old Ivy and Burgundy
- Metallic acrylic craft paint in Antique Gold
- Decoupage medium, antique
- Antiquing medium, brown
- Gold foil paper banding, 1 inch wide
- Scraps of Victorian-style wrapping papers
- Metallic wax finish in Classic Gold
- Floral wallpaper
- ½-inch stencil brush
- Foam brushes

How do you define Victorian style?

The Victorians believed ornament was not a luxury but a necessity. Their home décor tended to be heavy-handed, filled from top to bottom with large, opulent pieces of furniture, pattern upon pattern, and collections on tabletops, shelves, and walls. Though too overdone to please today's eye, touches of Victoriana can add visual interest, dressing up a plain room.

Directions

Make sure the boxes are dust- and lint-free. If you use wooden Shaker boxes instead of papier mâché ones, lightly sand them before painting.

Cover the two largest boxes with two coats of Burgundy paint. Paint the smallest box with two coats of Old Ivy paint. Let them dry.

Using the photo, above right, as a general guide, cut scraps and motifs from the wallpaper and the Victorian scrap papers. Following the directions for Paper Decoupage (page 48), secure the images on the lids and sides of the boxes with the antique decoupage finish, but don't cover the bands.

Arrange the gold foil around the banding of each box, and adhere it with the decoupage medium.

Following the directions for Rubbing a Gold Finish (page 47), massage gold wax along the edges of the boxes, applying as much or as little as you desire.

Lightly sponge over the boxes with the antiquing medium. To add a different texture, apply the antiquing medium with the stencil brush, pouncing and swirling the brush to create an uneven finish. Seal the box with at least two coats of decoupage medium.

Directions

Sand and prime the table and stool. When the primer is dry, apply two coats of Burgundy paint to the stool. Trim it with gold leaf. Base-coat the tabletop with the Licorice paint. Following the directions for Granite (page 45), apply the faux finish using the green and white paints. When all paint has dried, apply two coats of glossy sealer.

Measure around the table to determine how much fabric you'll need for the width of the skirt. If you only pleat the front, as this project illustrates, double the final measurement. Full pleats all around will require three times the original measurement. Add an inch for side hems. When measuring for length, allow for any desired drape in the skirt, and add 2 inches for bottom and top hems.

Cut out the fabric. Fold over the side edges ¹/₂ inch to the back, and sew them in place. Fold over the top edge 1 inch to the back side, and sew it in place. Fold over the lower edge 1 inch to the back side, adjusting length, and sew in place. Position the skirt around the dressing table, folding the pleats in place, and secure it with upholstery tacks.

Trace the seat on plain brown paper, and add 3 inches all around. Using this pattern, cut out several layers of batting and one piece of fabric. Position the batting on top of the stool seat, and staple it in place. Trim off any excess. Next, position the piece of fabric over the batting, folding excess under the seat where you'll staple it in place. Work from the center out toward the sides, smoothing wrinkles in the fabric and keeping the pattern straight. Measure the outside edge of the seat, and cut trim to fit. Apply the trim using fabric glue.

Dressing Table

You Will Need

- Dressing table and stool
- Acrylic primer
- Acrylic craft paint in Ivory White, Poetry Green, Aspen Green, Green Meadow, Old Ivy, Licorice, and Burgundy
- Sandpaper and tack cloth
- Natural sea sponge
- Paint extender
- Paint thickener
- Gold leaf paint
- Floral fabric
- Polyester quilt batting
- Upholstery tacks
- Solid-green fabric
- Decorative trim
- Staple gun
- Sewing machine
- Matching thread
- Measuring tape
- Iron
- Fabric glue
- Gloss and matte sealer

Cheval Mirror

You Will Need

- Unfinished pine full-length mirror
- Rosewood stain
- Leaf design rubber stamp
- Raised-surface ink stamp pad in Metallic Gold
- Metallic wax finish in Classic Gold
- Mineral spirits
- Kraft paper or newspaper
- Chalk pencil
- Masking tape
- Sandpaper and tack cloth
- Soft lint-free cloths
- Rubber gloves
- Sealer

What are the characteristics of Victorian-style furniture? Early pieces featured Gothic details. Eventually the massive scale and exaggerated curves evolved, especially in the forms of carved fruit and flowers. With mass production came the fancy wood scrollwork seen in the gingerbread trim and ornate hardware we recognize today. Vintage pieces abound, but reproductions are available, too.

Directions

Cover the glass with large sheets of paper. Secure the paper with tape. Sand the frame and stand, and wipe them clean with a tack cloth. If you aren't working with a new, unfinished piece, remove all of the old finish thoroughly before starting. The wood has to be porous to properly absorb the stain.

Wearing protective rubber gloves, apply the stain to the wood surfaces, following the grain, using a soft cloth. Wipe away any excess stain that is unabsorbed by the wood. To create a darker shade, add another coat. Allow the stain to dry for 24 hours.

Map out the placement of the leaf motif along the sides of the mirror, marking it lightly with a chalk pencil. Following the directions for Rubber Stamping (page 51), load Metallic Gold ink onto the leaf stamp, and apply it along the sides of the mirror, changing the direction of the design as desired. Reload the stamp as necessary. If you make a mistake, wipe off the ink with mineral spirits and reapply. Following the directions for Rubbing a Gold Finish (page 47), wipe gold wax along the bevels or edges of the frame. When all surfaces are dry, apply sealer. Remove the paper and polish the glass.

Folding Screen

You Will Need

- Three-panel wicker screen
- Metallic wax in Florentine Gold
- Spray paint
- in Dark Green
- Soft, lint-free cloth
- Diamond-shaped template (optional)
- Masking tape

Directions

Wicker, especially if it's old, needs a little TLC to keep it looking good. If your piece shows signs of age, such as damage to the weave, repair it before doing anything else. You can fix minor tears using wood glue. Avoid badly damaged pieces.

The dark green wicker screen featured in this project was purchased that way, but you can refinish any natural or white wicker piece with green spray paint. Working in a well-ventilated space and following the manufacturer's directions, hold the can 2 to 4 feet from the surface. Apply two coats of the paint to both sides of each of the panels. To get the paint evenly and thoroughly into all of the crevices, it's best to build up several layers of a fine mist. Avoid spraying too much paint at a time, which will cause drips. Let the paint dry.

Follow the directions for Rubbing a Gold Finish (page 47), and apply the metallic gold wax along any details, such as any spokes or edges of the screen. Draw a diamond-shape form to use as a guideline (see the photograph, above right). With the guide taped in place, work the gold wax onto the wicker with your finger.

How do you accessorize for Victorian style? Everything from stuffed birds to human-hair "paintings" found their way into authentic Victorian homes. These people loved the exotic, particularly chinoiserie, as well as their gardens and their pets. You can emulate this look with similarly themed framed prints, carpets, and knickknacks. Don't forget the Victorian mantra: There can never be too much of a good thing!

A Lush Garden Room

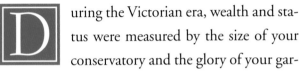

"And we've got to get ourselves back to the garden."—Joni Mitchell

During the Victorian era, wealth and status were measured by the size of your conservatory and the glory of your garden. Today people garden for pleasure, and while not everyone is lucky enough to have a conservatory in their home, it's easy and therapeutic to create the illusion of a garden room in a sunny corner or on a porch. By using a blend of summery elements, you can create an oasis even in the middle of winter. Doesn't everyone need a place of refuge in which to spend a few quiet moments?

The combination of fresh white wicker and cheerful floral fabrics are almost instant harbingers of spring. Choose a fabric pattern around which you would like to build your color scheme. The garden room featured in this chapter takes its color cues from a crisp cotton fabric with a design of bright pastel posies and blue-and-white checked ribbon accents. Flower motifs carefully cut out from fabric and applied to an inexpensive wicker chair lend a real summerhouse look. A coordinating paint color highlights the edges. The fabric decoupage technique works best on tightly woven wicker; if you're working with an antique, make sure the weave and finish are in good condition.

Sturdy unprimed canvas becomes a fabulous floor cloth with the use of real fern fronds as stencil patterns. An easy spray-paint technique transfers the image to the canvas.

Luscious paper bouquets transform an ordinary galvanized washbasin into an elegant container for magazines. You can use images of copyright-free antique botanical prints right out of a book. Most copy shops now have equipment that reproduces beautiful color images. You can easily have the image enlarged or reduced, too.

Octagonal glass plates, available at craft stores, become the canvas for flower cutouts and coordinating papers that tie into a colorful palette. The paper is applied to the underside of the plates, so you can use them for serving as long you can wipe them clean and don't submerge them in water.

Wicker Chair

How do you define garden style? Even if you live in the city, you can create a summery feeling by bringing nature indoors. The key elements of garden style are sunlight, nature motifs, and an abundance of plants. Furnish rooms with vintage garden and porch wares. Today, antique wicker, rattan, and wrought iron are in such demand that they are very costly and hard to find. Fortunately there are a lot of affordable new versions readily available. Rub new wicker with a wash of contrasting paint, and sand it down slightly, and it will look as good as old!

Directions

*U*nless you're working with a relatively new white chair, refresh its finish using White spray paint. Following the manufacturer's instructions and holding the can 2 to 4 feet from the project, spray a fine mist of paint evenly over the chair to cover it completely. Move the spray can back and forth to coat the chair thoroughly, but don't overload it with wet paint. Too much will result in drips, so let the finish build up gradually. When the first coat dries, go over the chair again. Apply two or three coats, as needed to get the paint adequately into the grooves and crevices, and always work in a well-ventilated space.

While the spray-paint dries, cut out motifs from the fabric; keep them to the side. Dip a damp sponge into a small amount of blue paint, blot it, and then rub the paint along edges of the chair to tint it slightly. Arrange the fabric cutouts on the back and along the front of the chair. Following directions for Fabric Decoupage (page 49), apply the cutouts; then coat the chair with sealer.

Fern Floor Cloth

Directions

Cut a 36- x 52-inch rectangle of heavyweight canvas. To create a neat hem, just fold over 1½ inches of the cloth on all four sides. Miter the cloth at the corners, and glue it to the underside. Cover a rolling pin with plastic wrap, and use it to smooth the hem in place. Finish with several coats of sealer. Paint the canvas with two or more coats of Poetry Green paint. Let it dry.

Using a ruler, measure and mark a 1-inch border around all four sides of the canvas. Before painting the border, run a line of masking tape along the edge next to the main section of the cloth, which you may also want to protect with newspaper. Following the directions for Sponging (page 51), lightly sponge enough yellow paint on the border to create contrast, but don't overdo the effect. Let it dry, and then remove the masking tape and paper.

Next, measure and mark a second, wider border that's 8 inches from the inside edge of the one you just painted. It should continue around all four sides of the canvas. With your ruler, draw an 8-inch square in each corner. Mask and cover both borders, except the corner squares.

Using spray adhesive, randomly mount the fern fronds in the corner squares and inside the main section of the cloth. Following directions for Negative Stenciling (page 40), spray these areas with Corn Silk paint. Let the paint dry; then remove the masking tape and the fronds. Apply sealer.

You Will Need

- Unprimed heavy-weight canvas
- Acrylic craft paint in Sunflower and Poetry Green
- Spray paint in Corn Silk
- Dried and pressed fern fronds
- Spray adhesive
- White glue
- Rolling pin
- Kraft paper or
- plastic wrap
- Flat foam paintbrushes
- Sponges, natural
- Masking or painter's tape
- Craft knife
- Paper towels
- Pencil
- Ruler or straightedge
- Scissors
- Sealer

Magazine Bucket

What colors, fabrics, and patterns look good with this style? Floral fabrics or ones with nature themes are the essence of garden style, whether they feature cheery primary colors or mellow faded tones on glazed chintzes or textured cloths. You can add variety with playful checks or stripes.

Directions

Following the manufacturer's instructions and holding the can 2 to 4 feet from the project, spray a fine mist of primer on the inside and outside surfaces of the bucket. Move the spray can back and forth to coat evenly and thoroughly. Work in a well-ventilated space. Try to get the paint into the crevices without overloading them. This will only cause drips that will mar your finish. Let each coat dry thoroughly before proceeding to the next.

Apply two coats of the pale yellow paint over the primed surfaces. Run masking tape along edges and handles of the bucket. Mix the neutral glaze with the Sage Green glaze until you have the desired shade. Following the directions for Ragging (page 36), paint the outside of the bucket with the mixture. Work one side of the bucket; then wait until it is dry before working the opposite side. Remove the masking tape.

Following the directions for Paper Decoupage (page 48), cut out the bouquets and affix them evenly spaced around the bucket. Apply two coats of sealer.

Following the directions for Rubbing a Gold Wax Finish (page 47), go over the edges and handles with gold wax sealer. You may want to mask the bucket beforehand. Once this dries, apply two coats of sealer.

Flower Plates

You Will Need

- 4 octagon-shaped glass plates
- Spray paint in White
- 4 different decorative gift-wrap papers: floral, check, gold, and nostalgia prints
- Decoupage medium
- Metallic gold marking pen
- Spray adhesive
- Flat foam paintbrushes
- Soft lint-free cloths
- Paper
- Pencil
- Craft knife
- Ruler or straightedge
- Scissors
- Tissue paper

Directions

Cut out the various motifs you'll be using for your project from the wrapping paper. Paint both sides of each cutout with decoupage medium, and allow them to dry. This will keep the edges crisp for easier application during the decoupage process.

First, cut out one floral design to fit in the center of each plate as well as a motif from the nostalgia-themed paper. Next, on tissue paper, trace one section of the rim of one of the plates, adding ⅛ inch all around. Use that to make a paper template. Trace it onto the back side of the checked paper, eight times for each plate. Then, adding ⅛ inch all around, trace the bottom of each plate, and cut out one piece of nostalgia paper to the same size. Cut a narrow strip of the gold paper to use as trim.

Position a floral cutout in the center of the underside of each plate, face down, and trace around it with the gold pen. Then make gold dots along the edges of the center. Following the directions for Paper Decoupage (page 48), apply the decoupage medium to the cutouts, and smooth them in place on the back of the plate with your finger, removing any air bubbles and wrinkles. Position the gold strips along the edges around the underside of the plate. Place the checked rim pieces one section at a time, overlapping the gold strips. Decoupage them in place, followed by the nostalgia cutouts.

Paint the back side of the plates with decoupage medium. To finish, spray a fine mist of White paint on the back of the plate to coat evenly and thoroughly.

A Child's Room

"The little world of childhood with its familiar surroundings is a model of the greater world."—Carl Jung

Children's rooms provide a safe haven where kids can escape from the adult world and venture into their own fantasy lands. They should be bright and upbeat with a touch of whimsy. For our example, a roll of charming wallpaper printed with a naive rendition of the Noah's Ark saga inspired a theme, with colors that are bold but not too bright and numerous images that add a graphic look to projects.

Every child's room needs plenty of storage, so an unfinished pine trunk makes an ideal toy chest that doubles as extra seating. The colors in the seat cushion's fabric inspired the palette for the multicolored blocks on the the trunk's front and side panels. To create it, all you need are some basic kitchen sponges and paint. A piece of 3-inch-thick foam, cut to size and covered with coordinating Noah's Ark fabric, pads the top, providing a comfortable seat for Mom or Dad to sit while reading bedtime stories.

The pint-sized table and chair feature cut-out animal and ark motifs that seem to float on brightly colored combed waves. Unfinished furniture stores are a good source for scaled-down tables, chairs, or chests—a must in little folks' rooms.

An unfinished wooden ark, complete with pairs of miniature animals, is a good find. It's fun to paint the animals either whimsically or realistically. The ark and its menagerie not only add to the visual theme but are unbreakable toys that will survive many rainy days.

Finally, when it comes to clutter, there are two schools of thought: to see or not to see. An open shelf puts everything on display, and the one featured in this room looks great with or without kids' trinkets, thanks to two easy decorative paint techniques, frottage and stenciling. Under-shelf pegs provide a neat spot to hang pajamas, a sweater or jacket, or a collection of hats.

Just about any novelty wallcovering with a graphic look and juvenile theme can be developed into a child's room motif. If Noah's Ark doesn't suit you, peruse the wallcovering books at your local paint store. From nursery rhymes to sports cars, one roll of wallpaper or a border can transform a dull room into a world of imagination.

Toy Chest

You Will Need

- Unfinished pine blanket chest
- Latex paint in off-white
- Acrylic craft paint in Sterling Blue, Cappuccino, and Dapple Gray
- Acrylic gloss paint in Laguna Blue
- Upholstery foam, 3 inches thick
- Noah's Ark-motif fabric
- Decorative trim
- Fabric glue
- Sharp serrated knife
- Staple gun
- Sandpaper and tack cloth
- Multipurpose primer
- Flat foam paintbrushes
- One cellulose sponge for each brick color
- Masking or painter's tape
- Craft knife
- Paper towels
- Chalk pencil
- Ruler or straightedge
- Scissors
- Sealer

Directions

Sand the trunk, and wipe it with a tack cloth. Apply two coats of primer, let it dry, and then follow with two coats of off-white paint. Let it dry.

Measure each side of the trunk, and divide the panels to establish a grid for sponge-block print with a small space between each block. A lot depends on the size of your sponge; you may need to cut sponge to fit. Mark the placement of the sponge blocks on the sides of the trunk with a chalk pencil and a straightedge, leaving about a 1/4-inch space between each one.

Because the blocks don't have to be perfectly aligned, use your eye to establish the spacing between each one. Following the directions for Sponging Blocks (page 52), apply the various paint colors randomly. Sterling Blue, Laguna Blue, Cappuchino, and Dapple Gray are the colors featured on the trunk above. Just in case your grid isn't perfect, start at the center; then continue to the right and left. That way, if your calculations come up a bit short, you can cheat on the size of the blocks at the end of the row. When it's dry, apply two coats of sealer.

To make the cushion, take a piece of fabric that's large enough to cover upholstery foam cut to fit the top of the trunk. Position the foam on the top of the trunk lid. Fold the fabric over the foam to the back side of the trunk top. Work from the center out toward the sides, smoothing wrinkles in the fabric and keeping the pattern straight, and staple it onto the lid. Miter the fabric at the corners of the trunk top. Finish by gluing trim along the edge of the trunk top.

You Will Need

- Unpainted wooden child's table and chairs
- Acrylic craft paint in Patina, Buttercup, Licorice, and Coffee Bean
- Decorator glaze in neutral and Plate Blue
- Noah's Ark stencil
- Noah's Ark-motif wallpaper
- Decoupage medium
- Rubber multipurpose paint comb
- Stencil brushes
- Spray adhesive
- Sandpaper and tack cloth
- Multipurpose primer
- Flat foam paintbrushes
- Sponges: natural
- Masking or painter's tape
- Craft knife
- Mixing container
- Paper towels
- Soft lint-free cloths
- Chalk pencil
- Ruler or straightedge
- Sharp-pointed scissors
- Sealer

Table and Chairs

Directions

Sand the table and chairs, and wipe them with a tack cloth. Apply one or more coats of primer, let it dry, then follow with two coats of Patina paint for the base. Let it dry.

Mix the neutral glaze with Plate Blue glaze until you get the desired shade. Use a sponge to apply an uneven coat of tinted glaze to the table and chair, including the legs. The green glaze that's applied to two of the chair's back spokes can be made by adding some of the Buttercup paint to the blue glaze mixture.

While the glaze is still wet and following the directions for Combing (page 31), use the paint comb to create the patterns. On the tabletop, work it in a wavy motion. On the chair seat, work it vertically, and then go over it again horizontally to make a checked pattern. On the flat back panel of the chair, comb alternating blocks of vertical and horizontal strokes. Let the glaze dry thoroughly.

Arrange the cut-out ark and animal motifs around the table and chairs, marking their placement with the chalk pencil; then apply them following the directions for Paper Decoupage (page 48).

Following the directions for Stenciling (page 39), add the words "Two by Two" with Licorice and Coffee Bean paints. Apply two coats of sealer to both pieces.

Ark Peg Shelf

You Will Need

- Unfinished wooden peg shelf, 24 inches wide
- Acrylic craft paint in Dark Gray, Terra Cotta, Cappuccino, Blue Ribbon, Evergreen, Wicker White, Buttercup, and Coffee Bean
- Noah's Ark stencil
- Stencil brushes
- Spray adhesive
- Newspaper or plastic wrap
- Sandpaper and tack cloth
- Multipurpose primer
- Flat foam paintbrushes
- Fine artist's paintbrushes
- Masking or painter's tape
- Craft knife
- Mixing containers
- Paper towels
- Pencil
- Ruler or straightedge
- Scissors
- Sealer

What is kid-proof style? Children tend to have strong opinions about color, ideas that don't always correspond with your own. Choose a palette that will please them, but fit in with the rest of your décor. Non-toxic odorless paints, particularly ones with special effects such as glitter, chalkboard, and glow-in-the-dark, can be fun and are easy to repaint over later. Scrubbable wallcoverings and stain-resistant laminate flooring are practical choices, too.

Directions

Remove the pegs from the shelf. Sand the shelf and the pegs; then wipe everything clean with a tack cloth. Apply primer, let it dry, and then follow with two coats of Cappuccino paint for the base. Let it dry.

Thin the blue paint with water. Following the directions for Frottage (page 35), coat the shelf with the thinned blue paint and work the technique, which adds a textured appearance. Rub the pegs with the thinned blue paint for an uneven finish.

Position the desired animal stencils across the shelf, and mark their placement; then follow the directions for Stenciling (page 39). Use Coffee Bean paint for the ark, Buttercup paint for the roof and the giraffe's body, and Terra Cotta paint for the animal's spots. The alligators should be rendered in Evergreen and the elephants in Dark Gray. Stencil the clouds with Wicker White paint. Let the paints dry, and then replace the pegs. Finish the piece with two or more coats of sealer.

You Will Need

- Unfinished wooden Noah's Ark and animals
- Acrylic craft paints in Portrait Light, White, Sunflower, Violet Pansy, Patina, Cappuccino, Tangerine, Red-violet, Azure Blue, Porcelain Blue, Lemonade, Buttercup, Harvest Gold, and Coffee Bean
- Acrylic gloss paint in Dolphin Gray, Black, and Brown
- Decorator glazes in neutral, Plate Blue, Sunflower, and Sage Green
- Standard paint comb
- French brush
- Stencil brush
- Sandpaper and tack cloth
- Multipurpose primer
- Flat foam paintbrushes
- Fine artist's paintbrushes: flat, liner, pointed, and round in assorted sizes
- Sponges, natural
- Masking or painter's tape
- Craft knife
- Mixing containers
- Paper towels
- Soft lint-free cloths
- Pencil
- Ruler or straightedge
- Sealer

Toy Boat

Directions

Sand all of the pieces, wipe them with a tack cloth, and then prime them. Base-coat the ark in Lemonade paint. Following the directions for Ragging (page 36) and using the Sunflower glaze, create a mottled surface on the top two-thirds of the ark. Paint the bottom third of the ark with Plate Blue glaze. Following the directions for Combing (page 31), make wavy lines. Paint the roof of the ark with Sage Green glaze; create a scalloped pattern with the comb. Paint the house Cappuccino; use Patina for its platform. Make two 1 x 1½-inch windows with Red-violet paint. Mix Red-violet and White paint for the line you'll paint around the edges of the ark. Paint cows White with Black spots. Paint zebras White. When they're dry, apply a mixture of Black paint and neutral glaze; pull through the wet glaze to create stripes. Leave a section unstriped for the mane. Pounce a french brush on wet Harvest Gold-painted camels for texture. Paint giraffes Sunflower with Coffee Bean spots. Mix Harvest Gold and Sunflower paints to decorate the lions. Create leathery elephant skin using a frottage effect (page 35) in Blue over Gray. Paint Noah and his wife any colors. Apply sealer to all.

Patterns

Follow the directions for Making Your Own Stencil (page 40), using these patterns as a guide. Enlarge or reduce these images on a copier to make them the correct scale for your project. To purchase ready-made stencils, see the Sources on page 126.

LETTERING

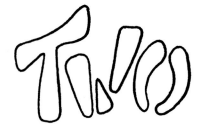  

RABBIT

CAMEL

BIRD

ARK

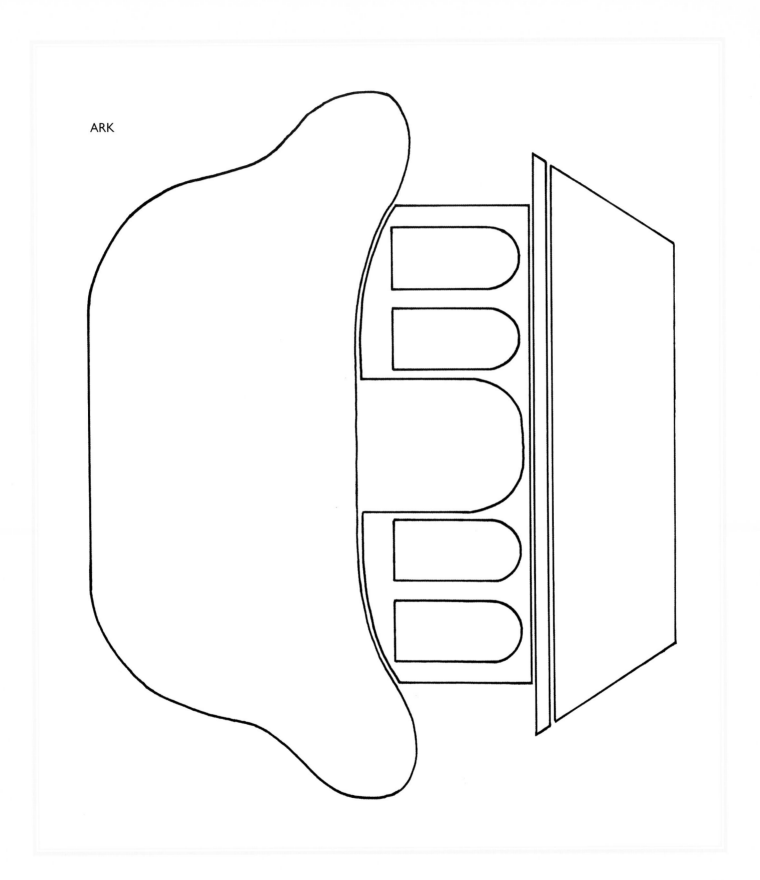

Patterns

ELEPHANT

ZEBRA

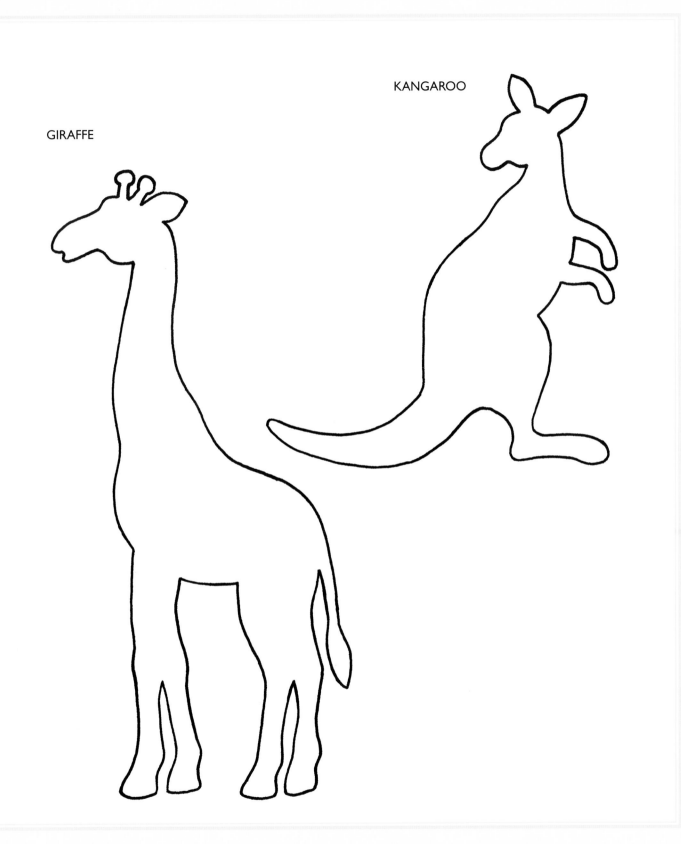

GIRAFFE

KANGAROO

A French-Country Dining Room

"My house here is painted the yellow color of fresh butter…And over it is the intensely blue sky." —Vincent van Gogh

The deep sky blue and warm sunflower yellow of a French country-style tablecloth inspired this dining room palette. The colors call to mind the hues Vincent van Gogh saw and painted while living in Provence. Their pairing takes advantage of the impact of color opposites: Warm and cool colors positioned side by side create exciting emotional and visual contrast.

For a country feeling, simple hand-painting techniques were used to make ordinary objects appear unique. Most of the motifs can be easily transferred to other things—for example, the simple flower-and-leaf pattern on the yellow chair would be a lovely decoration on a drawer front or cupboard door. The easy outlining technique ties the elements together and works especially well to create the cohesiveness required by small prints.

The idea for the olive design on the tabletop shelf comes directly from the tablecloth fabric. Outlined with an easy-to-paint border, it blends with the painted cupboard on which it sits.

The vine pattern gracing the serving tray is borrowed from a butter dish purchased in France. The oval metal tray itself was found in a thrift shop, but if you can't find a similar one, translate the design to any shape tray. Painted metal trays in perfect condition are too wonderful to paint over, but the rusty versions you can pick up cheaply at tag sales are easy to refinish with a good sanding and metal primer.

To complete the tabletop arrangement, a simple crackle technique transformed a group of plain wooden candlesticks into instant "antiques."

The design on the clock, which was made from components purchased at a craft store, can be applied to any flat, round surface.

The shape of a junk-shop chair was comely, but its condition was poor. Regluing the loose joints and filling gaps with wood putty helped turn it around. A few coats of yellow paint and a hand-painted decoration elevated it to folk art status.

Tabletop Shelf

You Will Need

- Unfinished table-top shelf
- Acrylic craft paint in True Blue, Ivory White, Sunflower, Brilliant Blue, Harvest Gold, and Sunny Yellow
- Decorator glaze in neutral
- Chalk pencil
- Plastic wrap
- Flat foam paintbrushes
- Sandpaper and tack cloth
- Pencil
- Transfer paper
- Artist's brushes, liner and medium round
- Sealer

How do you evoke French-country style with textiles?

Multicolored designs, particularly flowered, colored cotton miniprints and red, blue, or yellow-striped linens, are characteristic of the region. Also, look for lightweight cottons featuring fruits or herbs, or the classic *Toile de Jouy* cotton fabric that recounts the bucolic scenes of the French countryside.

Directions

S and the piece to create a smooth surface, and then wipe it with a tack cloth. Paint it with two coats of the Brilliant Blue paint. Let it dry.

Following the directions for Frottage (page 35), mix the neutral glaze with True Blue paint, and apply it with a foam brush. Work the finish over the surface of the shelf with plastic wrap. Let it dry.

Following the directions for Simple Hand Painting (page 37), create the olive design on the back of the top shelf. Mark the place for the design with a pencil.

Sketch the design freehand, or transfer it from a stencil. Use a combination of the Harvest Gold and Sunflower paints for the olives and leaves, highlighting with the Ivory White.

Using chalk, draw a narrow line down the center of the edge of the piece and each of the individual shelves. Using a liner brush, paint a narrow stripe over the line with the Sunny Yellow paint. Let it dry; then apply two or more coats of sealer over the entire surface.

Oval Tray

You Will Need

- Oval metal tray
- Metal primer
- Acrylic gloss enamel craft paint in White, Real Yellow, Real Green, Real Blue, Black, and Coffee Bean Brown
- Metallic wax finish
- in Classic Gold
- Foam brushes
- Artist's brushes
- Sandpaper and tack cloth
- Transfer paper
- Pencil
- Spray sealer

Directions

Sand the tray to create a smooth, clean surface, and then apply one or more coats of primer intended for metal surfaces. Let the primer dry.

Cover the tray with two or more coats of White paint. Following the directions for Simple Hand Painting (page 37), sketch your design in pencil. You can draw it freehand, using the one in the photograph, above right, as a guide, or trace and transfer a stencil motif if you prefer.

Using a script-liner paintbrush, make the squiggly lines with black paint and the flower petals with Real Blue paint. Create the center of the flower with a dab of Real Yellow paint. Accent that with a tiny dot using a small round paintbrush and Coffee Bean Brown paint. Use the Real Green paint for the leaves. Finish this section of the tray by painting a black squiggly line around the edges, as shown in the photograph. Paint the rim of the tray Real Blue.

Following the directions for Rubbing a Gold Finish (page 47), smudge gold wax along the edges; then finish the tray with two coats of spray sealer.

*How do you recognize **French country-style furniture?** Look for chunky farm-style tables, cupboards, hutches, and armoires made of darker woods, such as polished walnut and other sturdy fruit-woods, chairs with rush seats, and painted and polychromed pieces, with naturalistic carvings and handsome hammered metal hinges and handles.*

109

Candlesticks

How
*do you create French-
country style with color?* When
you think of French-country style, picture Provence and the sun-drenched colors
found there. Particularly look at nature—the
purple-blue sea of a hill of lavender or a cluster
of wisteria hanging over an iron grill, liquidy gold
wheat fields, lush bouquets of yellow sunflowers,
the delicate whiteness of almond blossoms, the
black flesh of a truffle, not to mention the red
ochre of the natural clay tiles and the bleached
gray stone walls and limestone hearths of the
old peasant houses. For more color inspiration, refer to fabric samples, travel
books, and the works of
van Gogh.

You Will Need

- Unfinished wood candlesticks in two sizes
- Latex paint in bright yellow
- Acrylic craft paint in Blue Ribbon
- Decorator glaze in Tuscan Sunset and Bluebell
- Flat foam paintbrushes
- Crackle medium
- Natural sponge
- Sandpaper and tack cloth
- Sealer

Directions

Sand the candlesticks to create a smooth surface, and then wipe them with a tack cloth. Following the example in the photograph, above right, apply two coats of bright yellow latex paint to the taller candlesticks, and two coats of Blue Ribbon craft paint to the shorter one. Let the paint dry.

Following the directions for Crackle Glazing (page 32), apply the crackle medium. To achieve a slightly crackled appearance, use a thin coat. For wider cracks, apply a thicker coating. Monitor the drying time of the crackle medium. Don't let it dry completely. While it's still tacky, apply the Bluebell glaze over the taller candlesticks; then go over the shorter candlestick with the Tuscan Sunset glaze. Apply this top coat with a natural sponge or a flat foam paintbrush, as desired. The sponge will give the candlesticks a slightly more worn look. After the top coat dries, protect the finish with two or more coats of sealer.

You Will Need

- Unfinished wooden clock plate, 9½-inch diameter
- Clock movement with hands
- Self-adhering clock face
- Acrylic gloss enamel paint in White, Real Yellow, Real Green, and Real Blue
- Artist's paintbrushes, #4 script liner and small round
- Flat foam paintbrushes
- Pencil
- Sandpaper and tack cloth

Directions

 and the plate to create a smooth surface, and then wipe it with a tack cloth. Apply two coats of White paint to the surface with a flat foam brush. Let it dry. Leaving the rim White, paint the center of the plate Real Yellow; then trim the edge with the same color.

With the pencil, draw a scallop design around the rim of the plate. Near the edge and in the center of each of the loops in the scallop, draw a small half circle about the size of a quarter. (See the photograph, above right.) Follow this with another scallop design, which should crisscross the first one around the entire rim. If you don't want to draw the scallops freehand, use the edge of a small plate or saucer as a guide.

Following directions for Simple Hand Painting (page 37), apply Real Blue paint with the liner brush to make wavy lines over the first of the scallop motifs and around the small half circle. Let the paint dry.

The second scallop will be the basis of the vine motif, which entails hand painting a small Real Yellow flower at the center of each scallop using a small round brush. Make leaves with the Real Green paint and the liner brush; use Real Blue paint for the line that connects them. Paint a blue dot inside the small half circle where the vines meet in a point. Let the paint dry.

Cut out the center section of the paper clock face so that the middle of the plate is exposed. Apply the self-adhering clock face. Hand paint a wreath in the center of the plate to match the vine. Accent with blue dots and triangles. When it's dry, apply sealer. Finally, attach the clock's hands and the movement mechanism.

Sunshine Chair

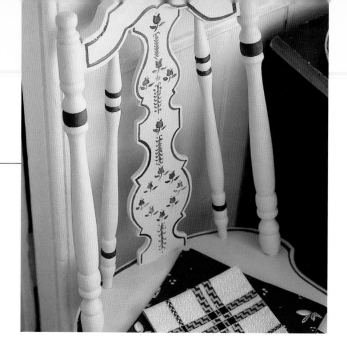

You Will Need

- Old wooden chair
- Wood filler
- Sandpaper and tack cloth
- Heavy-duty primer
- Latex paint in bright yellow
- Acrylic craft paint
- in True Blue
- Artist's paintbrushes, #4 script liner and small-point round
- Pencil
- Chalk pencil

What other accessories evoke a French-country mood? Airy lace curtains, pots of brightly colored flowering plants, faience pottery, and printed linens are some easy-to-acquire accessories that can set the tone. You can also hang copper pots or create a display on a baker's rack. Install a wrought-iron chandelier. If you can't afford a pricey cast-iron stove, invest in a handsome copper range hood accented with earthenware tiles.

Directions

Tighten or glue any loose joints in the chair, and clamp them. Fill any small gaps or cracks with wood filler as needed. Allow these repairs to dry overnight before removing the clamps. Smooth the surface with a light sanding; then wipe it with a tack cloth.

Apply two coats of primer. Let it dry before painting the chair with two coats of bright yellow latex paint.

Once the paint dries, use a chalk pencil to sketch the flower and leaf design on the carved center panel in the back of the chair, as well as the thin line that will outline the seat and the back panels. The small tulips and leaves are easy to make freehand with just a few brushstrokes, or copy the stencil pattern, opposite.

Following directions for Simple Hand Painting (page 37) and using the fine paintbrushes and True Blue paint, color in the design, and go over the outline. Highlight some of the turned spokes in blue, as well. Let the paint dry, and then apply two coats of sealer.

Follow the directions for Making Your Own Stencil (page 40) using these patterns as a guide. Enlarge or reduce these images on a copier to make them the correct scale for your project. To purchase ready-made stencils, see the Sources on page 126.

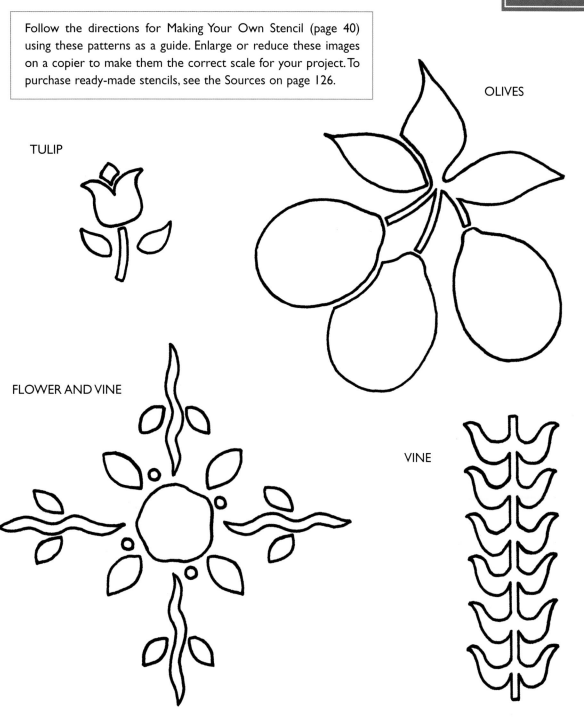

OLIVES

TULIP

FLOWER AND VINE

VINE

A Welcoming Country Kitchen

"The most important room in a house, to me, is the kitchen."—Alice Waters

The expression, "the kitchen is the heart of the house," is repeated often because it's true. Even when you plan to entertain your guests in the living room, where does everyone always end up? And where do you sit with your closest pals to chat over a cup of tea? Where do the kids do their homework? That's right, it's the kitchen, a room that's a magnet of hospitality, comfort, and warmth—and the source of the wonderful aroma of good food.

So why not enhance the welcoming ambiance with a kitchen decorating theme gathered around the bountiful fruits of the harvest? The bold shapes and bright hues of vegetables and fruits inspired the projects in this chapter. You'll notice that a warm palette was chosen for the base coat of most of the accessories to underscore the theme. A checkerboard pattern repeated throughout adds a strong visual element and serves as a cohesive component to tie all of the projects together.

Carrots, cabbage, and celery depicted in a novelty wallcovering of robust vegetables provide images for a trio of stools. You can purchase inexpensive unfinished pine versions and treat them with an easy-to-paint gingham-check technique. After enlarging the vegetable motifs at a copy shop, just apply them to the seats and finish them with several coats of sealer so that they will be sure to stand up to all the use they are bound to get. When you're finished, compare them to similar versions in pricey catalogs; you'll be delighted with the savings.

Another practical and pretty project is the wooden tool caddy transformed by paint and stencils into a handy tabletop container. Filled with flatware, napkins, and condiments, it's a fun accessory that keeps kitchen clutter to a minimum.

Coordinating stencils extend the harvest theme to a hinged bread box, a painted wall shelf, and tiles. Hand-painted details add realism, and special paints add a glazed look to the unfinished tiles.

Vegetable Stools

You Will Need

- 3 unfinished wooden kitchen stools
- Latex paint in Linen White
- Acrylic craft paint in Sterling Green, Poppy Red, and Mystic Green
- Decoupage medium
- Vegetable-print motifs from wallpaper or decorative paper
- Flat foam paintbrushes
- Sandpaper and tack cloth
- Masking or painter's tape
- Craft knife
- Ruler or straightedge
- Sponge, natural or cellulose
- Pencil
- Cardboard tube from paper towel roll
- Sealer

How can you give your kitchen a facelift? You don't need a big budget or professional assistance to add new style to your kitchen. Because in most households kitchens get more use than any other room, they need frequent sprucing up. Even with regular cleaning, kitchen surfaces get caked with grease, which attracts dust and grime after just a few years of normal living. While it's impractical to do a complete overhaul every few years, it's easy to make relatively simple changes. New paint, wallpaper, cabinet hardware, and window treatments can add a refreshing face to a kitchen at an affordable price.

Directions

Sand the kitchen stools to create a smooth surface, and wipe them with a tack cloth. After priming the stools, paint them entirely with two coats of the Linen White paint. Let the paint dry.

Following the directions for Painting Stripes and Plaid (page 36), mask and apply the technique, using a different shade of the acrylic paint for each stool seat.

Following the directions for Paper Decoupage (page 48), cut out and apply vegetable motifs to the seats.

To create a scalloped border, pour a small amount of the Linen White paint onto a paper plate. Dip half of one end of a cardboard tube into the paint. Using the photo above as a guide and the tube as a stamp, transfer the paint to the stools, reloading when necessary and working the design all the way around each of the seat tops. When the paint is dry, finish the stools with two or more coats of sealer.

Silverware Caddy

You Will Need

- Unfinished wooden tool caddy
- Acrylic craft paint in Crimson, Buttercream, Poetry Green, Red Orange, and Harvest Gold
- Fruit stencils
- Foam sponges
- Flat foam paintbrushes
- Sandpaper and tack cloth
- Pencil
- Artist's liner brush
- Sealer

Directions

You don't have to have an old wooden tool caddy for your project. In fact, it's easier to work with a new, unfinished version, which you can purchase at a craft shop. Either way, make sure the wood is dirt-free, but go over the edges with sandpaper to create a slightly distressed vintage appearance.

Next, apply two coats of the Buttercream paint to both the outside and interior sections of the caddy. Let the paint dry.

Following the directions for Sponging Blocks (page 52), apply a small checkerboard pattern along the sides and handle using the Harvest Gold paint. Following the directions for Stenciling (page 39), create the fruit motif using the red and green paints. With an artist's brush, apply a thin green line freehand along the edges of the handle. Finish with two coats of sealer.

How can you add warmth to a contemporary-style kitchen? Clean modern materials, such as stainless steel, cast concrete, and granite, are ideally suited to kitchen surfaces because they're so hard-wearing. However, they can make a kitchen appear cold. To avoid a sterile feeling in a contemporary kitchen, counterbalance these sleek materials with wood and color. Even if your prefer a neutral color scheme, choose a warm shade, one with a slightly yellow cast.

Bread Box

You Will Need

- Unfinished wooden hinged-lid bread box
- All-purpose primer
- Acrylic craft paint in Purple, Crimson, Poetry Green, Lemon Custard, Harvest Gold, Sunny Yellow, and Burnt Sienna
- Decorator glaze in Sunflower
- Fruit border stencil
- Small foam sponge
- Artist's brushes: #3 round and ½-inch flat
- Dragging brush
- Flat foam paintbrushes
- Pencil
- Sandpaper and tack cloth
- Sealer

Directions

Sand the bread box to create a smooth surface, and wipe it with a tack cloth. Mask the hinges, and then prime the box. When the primer is dry, apply two coats of Lemon Custard paint. Let it dry.

Following the directions for Dragging (page 34), apply the technique using the Sunflower glaze. Let it dry.

Transfer the fruit motif to the lid of the bread box using the assorted acrylic paints and following the directions for Hand Painting from a Stencil (page 38). Refer to the photo, above right, as a guide for positioning.

To create the checkerboard pattern, follow the directions for Sponging Blocks (page 52), and apply the pattern along the edge of the box with Burnt Sienna paint. Finish with two or more coats of sealer.

How can you create a country-kitchen look? The key to a country kitchen is coziness and a down-to-earth sensibility. This is easy to attain with wood floors and cabinets either left natural or painted and distressed. Besides the traditional American-country classic, there's the cheerful look of Vintage style, which uses graphic patterns and colors from the 1930s, '40s, and '50s. Terrific old kitchen linens, Fiestaware, and retro appliances pull the look together. French-, Italian-, and English-country styles offer another approach for those with a taste for something different. Many of our own cooking traditions have their origins in Old World cuisine, so it's only natural to turn to our continental cousins for design tips, such as making a fabulous range the focal point of the kitchen and using lots of tile and stone surfaces around the room.

Three-Tile Shelf

Directions

Sand the shelf, and then wipe it with a tack cloth. Apply two coats of Buttercrunch paint. Let it dry. Pour a small amount of each of the remaining acrylic paints into a paint palette. Dip the stippling brush into the paints, and dab lightly on a paper towel to remove excess paint. Lightly pounce the brush up and down on all sides of the shelf to create a fine-textured, multicolored surface, allowing the base coat to show through. Allow the paint to dry. Following the directions for Sponging Blocks (page 52), create a small checkered pattern all along the edges of the shelf using the Burnt Sienna paint.

Next, go over the tiles with surface cleaner and a lint-free cloth. Using Yellow ceramic paint and referring to the directions for Sponging Blocks once again, apply a checkered border along the edges of each tile.

Place a fruit stencil (pages 120-122) in the center of each tile, and secure it in place with spray adhesive. Following the directions for Stenciling (page 39), paint a different fruit on each tile. Add dimension with shading. Apply lighter colors toward the center of each fruit. Paint the tiles with two or more coats of the glaze. Coat the tiles with sealer. When sealer dries, glue the tiles in place on the back of the shelf with the tile adhesive.

Patterns

Follow the directions for Making Your Own Stencil (page 40), using these patterns as a guide. Enlarge or reduce these images on a copier to make them the correct scale for your project. To purchase ready-made stencils, see the Sources on page 126.

LARGE APPLE

PLUMS

LARGE PEAR

CHERRIES

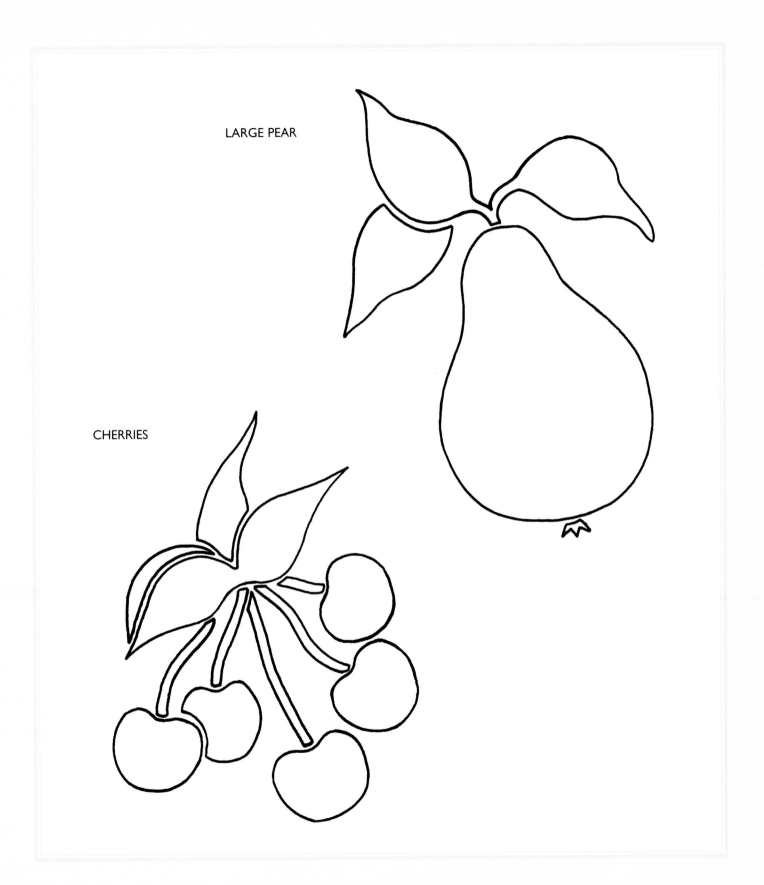

Patterns

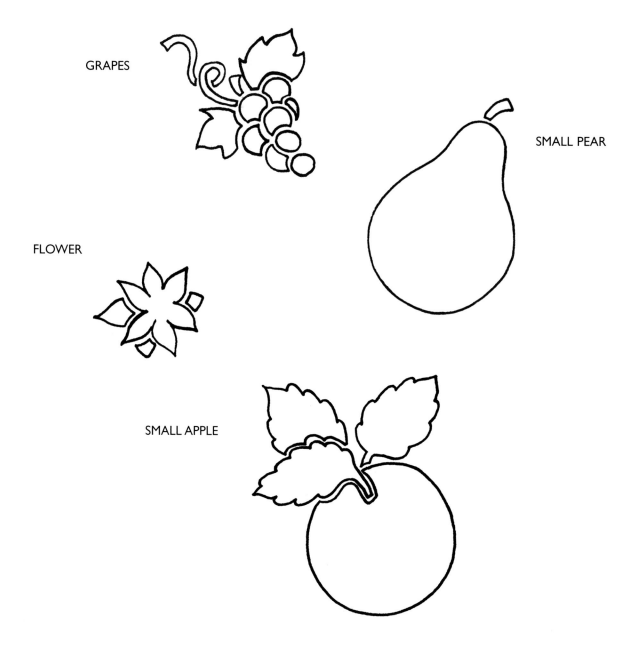

GRAPES

SMALL PEAR

FLOWER

SMALL APPLE

FRUIT BORDER

Glossary

Acetate: The plastic sheet material often used for making stencils.

Acrylic paint: A water-soluble paint with a plastic polymer (acrylic) binder.

Alkyd paint: A paint-thinner-soluble paint that contains a binder made of soya or urethane resins (alkyds). It is often imprecisely called "oil-based" paint. Alkyds have replaced linseed oil, which was used as a binder in oil-based paint.

Aniline dyes: Any of numerous synthetic dyes. Aniline dyes were developed in Germany in 1856.

Artist's oil paint: Paint that consists of pigment suspended in linseed oil. It comes in a tube and in a wide range of saturated colors.

Blender brushes: Specialty brushes used to blend and soften all types of wet painted surfaces.

Cheesecloth: A loosely woven, coarse cotton gauze used to create

different textures as well as to blend and smooth wet paint over a surface.

Cheesecloth distressing: The technique of blending and softening wet paint strokes and colors by pouncing bunched-up cheesecloth over a surface.

Clear top coat: A transparent finishing layer of protection applied over a decorated surface.

Color scheme: A group of colors used together to create visual harmony in a space.

Color washing: The technique of applying layers of heavily thinned glaze to a surface to produce a faded, transparent wash of color.

Combing: A technique that involves dragging a plastic or metal comb through wet paint or glaze in order to simulate texture or to create a pattern.

Contrast: The art of assembling colors with different values and intensities and in different proportions to create a dynamic scheme.

Decoupage: The technique of applying cut-out paper or fabric motifs to a surface, and then coating the images with varnish or decoupage medium.

Decoupage medium: A smooth and glossy gluelike liquid used to

apply cut-out paper or fabric images to a surface or an object. It is used as both an adhesive and a top coat.

Dragging: A technique that involves pulling a special long-bristled brush through wet paint or glaze to create fine lines or narrow stripes.

Faux: The French word for "false." With regard to painted finishes, it is used to describe any technique in which paint is manipulated on a surface to imitate the appearance of another substance, such as wood or stone.

Ferrule: The metal part of a paintbrush that holds the bristles to the handle.

Flat finish: The absence of sheen after a paint or finish dries.

Flogger/dragger: A wide, long-bristled brush that can be dragged through or slapped over wet paint or glaze to simulate texture or to create a pattern.

Glaze: A thinned-down, translucent emulsion that may or may not contain pigment (color).

Glossy finish: The appearance of sheen after a paint or finish dries.

Graining comb: A flexible steel or plastic device with random-sized tines or teeth. It is dragged through wet glaze or paint to create striated or grained surfaces. A common hair comb makes a workable substitute.

Latex paint: Paint that contains either acrylic or vinyl resins or a combination of the two. High-quality latex paints contain 100-percent acrylic resin. Latex paint is water-soluble and dries quickly.

Lining brush: A thin, flexible, long-bristled brush used for fine lining and detail work.

Mottler: A flat-ended brush used to make woodlike texture in glazed surfaces.

Negative stenciling: Creating an image or a motif on a surface, often in a repeated pattern, by applying a form and then painting around it. The shape of the image remains on the surface after the form is removed. See also Positive stenciling.

Negative technique: Any painting technique that involves removing wet paint or glaze from a surface. See also Positive technique.

Overglaze: A thin glaze added as a final step to a decorative finish. It can be a thinner version of the base coat or one mixed in a different color.

Palette: Traditionally, a small wooden board for mixing dollops of paint. It can also be made of plastic or improvised using a glass, plastic, or plastic-coated-paper plate.

Palette knife: An artist's knife with a thin, dull, flexible blade, used for mixing, scraping, or applying paint. It can be made of plastic or metal.

Polyurethane: A tough, hard-wearing coating made of synthetic resins. It serves as a good top coat or

finish and can be applied over most types of paint, except artist's oils.

Positive stenciling: Creating an image or a motif, often in a repeated pattern, by painting a cut-out pattern.

Positive technique: Any painting technique that involves applying paint to a surface. See also Negative technique.

Primers: Primers prepare surfaces for painting by making them more uniform in texture and giving tooth.

Ragging off: The technique in which paint is pulled from a surface with a bunched-up cloth. Sometimes called "cheeseclothing."

Ragging on: The technique in which paint is applied to a surface with a bunched-up cloth.

Registration marks: Small holes cut into a stencil with more than one layer, which allow you to match up the different layers.

Sea sponge: A natural sponge, not to be confused with the cellulose variety used in households.

Sealers: These seal porous surfaces by forming a durable, non-absorbent barrier that prevents them from sucking up paint.

Semigloss finish: These paints have a hard, slightly glossy finish that is light reflective, somewhere between gloss and eggshell.

Shade: A color to which black has been added to make it darker.

Sheen: The quality of paint that reflects light when it is dry.

Spattering: Applying random dots of paint over a surface by striking a saturated brush or by rubbing paint through a screen.

Sponging: A paint technique that involves using a sponge to apply or take off paint.

Stencil: A cut-out pattern.

Stipplers: Blocky, stiff-bristled hog-hair brushes used to stipple wet paints, glazes, and top coats.

Stippling: A paint technique that involves pouncing a brush over a surface, creating myriad tiny dots.

Thinner: A liquid that is mixed with paint to make it less thick. Mineral spirits may be used for alkyd paints and water for latex paint.

Tint: A color to which white has been added to make it lighter.

Tone: A color to which gray has been added to change its value.

Trompe l'oeil: French for "fool the eye"—used to describe a painted surface that convincingly mimics reality.

Wash: A thinned-out latex or acrylic paint.

Sources

A Lovely Living Room *(pp. 56-67)*

Mantel Planter: Off-white **satin-finish latex paint**; *Solid Gold* and *Solid Bronze FolkArt Metallics* **acrylic paint** from Plaid Enterprises; **diamond** and **line border stencil** from Plaid Enterprises; **star stamp** from Rubber Stampede. Topiary Fireplace Screen: Off-white **satin-finish latex paint**; *Solid Gold* and *Antique Gold FolkArt Metallics* **acrylic paint** from Plaid Enterprises; *Neutral, Italian Sage, Russet Brown, Sage Green, Ivy Green, Deep Woods Green,* and *Patina* **decorator glazes** from Plaid Enterprises; **lattice, rope border,** and **urn stencils** from Plaid Enterprises; **ivy decorator block** from Plaid Enterprises; **decor scroll stamp** from Rubber Stampede; *Apple Butter Brown* **antiquing medium** from Plaid Enterprises; *Classic Gold* **liquid leaf** from Plaid Enterprises. Marbled End Table: **Unfinished Shaker-style table (#8057)** from Mastercraft; Off-white **satin-finish latex paint**; *French Vanilla, Wicker White, Dapple Gray,* and *Caramel FolkArt Colors* **acrylic paint** from Plaid Enterprises; *Tuscan Sunset* and *Russet Brown* **decorator glazes** from Plaid Enterprises; **paint extender** from Plaid Enterprises; **paint thickener** from Plaid Enterprises; *Gold Classic* **metallic wax finish** from Plaid Enterprises. Table Lamp and Shade: *French Vanilla, Antique Gold,* and *Old Ivy FolkArt Metallics* **acrylic paint** from Plaid Enterprises; *Russet Brown, Sage Green, Deep Woods Green,* and *Patina* **decorator glazes** from Plaid Enterprises; **ivy decorator block** from Plaid Enterprises; **lattice stencil** from Plaid Enterprises; *Wood'n Bucket Brown* **antiquing medium** from Plaid Enterprises; *Classic Gold* **liquid leaf** from Plaid Enterprises; **unfinished pine lamp base** from Mill Store Products; **Unfinished wooden lamp base (#1064)** from Mill Store Products; **self-adhesive lampshade** from Hollywood Lights; **topiary fabric** from Waverly.

A Bedroom to Dream In *(pp. 68-75)*

Headboard: Green **satin-finish latex paint**; *Cappuccino, Poetry Green, Green Meadow,* and *Taffy FolkArt Colors* **acrylic paints** from Plaid Enterprises; *Mary Rosie* **wallcovering** from the *Vintage Rosie Collection* by Motif Designs; *Renaissance Gold* **metallic wax finish** from Plaid Enterprises; *Royal Coat* **decoupage medium** from Plaid Enterprises. Side Chair: Off-white **satin-finish latex**

paint; *Poetry Green* and *Aspen Green FolkArt Colors* **acrylic paint** from Plaid Enterprises; *Light Red Oxide* **artist's pigment** from Plaid Enterprises; *Mary Rosie* **fabric** from the *Vintage Rosie Collection by Motif Designs*. Tin Pitcher: *Eggshell* and *Beachcomber Apple Barrel Acrylics* **gloss enamel paint** from Plaid Enterprises; *Solid Bronze FolkArt Metallics* **acrylic paint** from Plaid Enterprises; **oval template** from Plaid Enterprises; *Royal Coat* **decoupage medium** from Plaid Enterprises; *Copper* **metallic wax finish** from Plaid Enterprises. Serving Tray: *Soft Green* **spray** paint from Krylon; *Mary Rosie* **fabric** from the *Vintage Rosie Collection* by Motif Designs. Dresser: **Three-drawer pine dresser (#9173)** from Mastercraft; *Cream* and *green* **satin-finish latex paint**; *Portrait Light, Naphthol Green, Poetry Green, Mystic Green, Old Ivy,* and *Burgundy FolkArt Colors* **acrylic paint** from Plaid Enterprises.

A Gentleman's Study *(pp. 76-83)*

Desk Mat: *Royal Coat* **decoupage medium** from Plaid Enterprises. Malachite Box: *Brick Red* and *Robin's Egg Green FolkArt Colors* **acrylic paint** from Plaid Enterprises; *Dark Green* **decorator glaze** from Plaid Enterprises; *Renaissance Gold* **metallic wax finish** from Plaid Enterprises. Bookends: *Brick Red FolkArt Colors* **acrylic paint** from Plaid Enterprises; *Renaissance Foil* **gold leafing sheets** from Delta Paints. Lamp: **Paper lampshade** from Kiti, a div. of Wire Works; *Patina* and *Old Ivy FolkArt Colors* **acrylic paint** from Plaid Enterprises; *Antique Copper* and *Solid Bronze FolkArt Metallics* **acrylic paint** from Plaid Enterprises; *Classic Gold* **metallic wax finish** from Plaid Enterprises. Desk Caddy: **Fleur-de-lis stamp** from Plaid Enterprises.

A Victorian Dressing Room *(pp. 84-89)*

Dressing Table and Stool: *Ivory White, Poetry Green, Aspen Green, Green Meadow, Old Ivy, Licorice* and *Burgundy FolkArt Colors* **acrylic paint** from Plaid Enterprises; **paint extender** from Plaid Enterprises; **paint thickener** from Plaid Enterprises; **liquid leaf** from Plaid Enterprises; *Morris Tapestry in Crimson* **fabric** from the *Victoria and Albert Collection* by Eisenhart. Storage Boxes: **Papier mâché boxes** from DCC;

Old Ivy and *Burgundy FolkArt Colors* **acrylic paint** from Plaid Enterprises; *Antique Gold FolkArt Metallics* **acrylic paint** from Plaid Enterprises; *Antique Royal Coat* **decoupage medium** from Plaid Enterprises; *Wooden Bucket Brown* **antiquing medium** from Plaid Enterprises; *Gold Classic* **metallic wax finish** from Plaid Enterprises; *Victorian Papers/Victorian Scraps* **images** from Plaid Enterprises; **gold foil banding** from Artifacts, Inc.; *Morris Tapestry in Crimson* **wallcovering** and **border** from the *Victoria and Albert Collection* by Eisenhart. Privacy Screen: *Florentine Gold* **metallic wax finish** from Plaid Enterprises; **three-panel wicker screen (#01658)** from the Home Decorator's Collection. Mirror: **Unpainted pine cheval mirror (#5000)** from Mastercraft; **leaf stamp** from Plaid Enterprises; **gold-ink stamp pad** from Rubber Stampede; *Classic Gold* **metallic wax finish** from Plaid Enterprises.

A Lush Garden Room
(pp. 90-95)

Magazine Bucket: Pale yellow **enamel paint**; *Sage Green* and *neutral* **decorator glazes** from Plaid Enterprises; *Classic Gold* **metallic wax finish** from Plaid Enterprises; *Royal Coat* **decoupage medium** from Plaid Enterprises. Wicker Chair: *Bluebell FolkArt Colors* **acrylic paint** from Plaid Enterprises. *Royal Coat* **decoupage medium** from Plaid Enterprises. Floor Cloth: **Unprimed canvas** from The Stencil Studio; *Cornsilk* **spray paint** from Krylon; *Sunflower* and *Poetry Green FolkArt Colors* **acrylic paint** from Plaid Enterprises.

A Child's Room (pp. 96-105)

Table and Chair Set: **Unpainted table and chairs** from Mastercraft; *Patina, Buttercup, Licorice,* and *Coffee Bean FolkArt Colors* **acrylic paint** from Plaid Enterprises; *Plate Blue* and *neutral* **decorator glazes** from Plaid Enterprises; *Noah and Company* **stencils** from Plaid Enterprises; *L'Arque de Paloma* **wallcovering** from Motif Designs; *Royal Coat* **decoupage medium** from Plaid Enterprises; **rubber painting comb** from Plaid Enterprises. Toy Chest: **Unpainted blanket chest (#1622)** from Mastercraft; Off-white

latex paint; *Sterling Blue, Cappucino* and *Dapple Gray FolkArt Colors* **acrylic paint** from Plaid Enterprises; *Laguna* **gloss-finish enamel paint** from Plaid Enterprises; *L'Arque de Paloma* **fabric** from Motif Designs. Shelf: **Unfinished, wooden pegged shelf, 24 inches wide (#8636)** from Walnut Hollow; *Dark Gray, Terra Cotta, Cappucino, Blue Ribbon, Evergreen, Wicker White, Buttercup* and *Coffee Bean FolkArt Colors* **acrylic paint** from Plaid Enterprises; *Noah and*

Company **stencils** from *Plaid Enterprises.* Ark: Unpainted **Noah's Ark and Animals (#BC101)** from Wood To Paint; *Portrait Light, White, Sunflower, Violet Pansy, Patina, Cappucino, Tangerine, Red Violet, Azure Blue, Porcelain Blue, Lemonade, Buttercup, Harvest Gold,* and *Coffee Bean FolkArt Colors* **acrylic paint** from Plaid Enterprises; *Dolphin Gray, Black,* and *Brown* **gloss-finish acrylic paint** from Plaid Enterprises; *Plate Blue, Sunflower, Sage Green,* and *neutral* **decorator glazes** from Plaid Enterprises.

A French-Country Dining Room (pp. 106-113)

Tray: *White, Real Yellow, Real Green, Real Blue, Black,* and *Coffee Bean Brown* **gloss-finish enamel paint** from Plaid Enterprises; *Classic Gold* **metallic-wax finish** from Plaid Enterprises. Chair: *True Blue FolkArt Colors* **acrylic paint** from Plaid Enterprises; Bright yellow **latex paint.** Candlesticks: **Wooden candlesticks** from Wood to Paint; Bright yellow **latex paint**; *Blue Ribbon FolkArt Colors* **acrylic paint** from Plaid Enterprises. *Tuscan Sunset* and *Blue Bell* **decorator glazes** from Plaid Enterprises; **crack-**

le medium from Plaid Enterprises. Clock: **Chippendale clock plate (#53219), clock movement with hands (#TQ-700P),** and **arabic clock face (medium, #116)** from Walnut Hollow; *White, Real Yellow, Real Green, Real Blue* **gloss-finish enamel paint** from Plaid Enterprises. Shelf: **Rustic storage shelf (#11-1806)** from Provo Craft; *True Blue, Ivory White, Sunflower, Brilliant Blue, Harvest Gold,* and *Sunny Yellow FolkArt Colors* **acrylic paint** from Plaid Enterprises; *neutral* **decorator glaze** from Plaid Enterprises.

A Welcoming Country Kitchen (pp. 114-123)

Bread Box: **Hinged-lid bread box (#MS110)** from Wood to Paint; *Purple, Crimson, Poetry Green, Lemon Custard, Harvest Gold, Sunny Yellow,* and *Burnt Sienna FolkArt Colors* **acrylic paint** from Plaid Enterprises; *Sunflower* **decorator glaze** from Plaid Enterprises; **fruit border** and **small checkerboard stencil** from Plaid Enterprises. Shelf: **What-not shelf** from Walnut Hollow; *French Vanilla, Crimson, Caramel, Buttercrunch, Buttercup,* and *Burnt Sienna FolkArt Colors* **acrylic paint** from Plaid Enterprises; **Lemons, plums,** and **oranges stencil** from Delta Paints; **small checkerboard stencil** from Plaid Enterprises; *CeramDecor* **surface cleaner** and **conditioner** from Delta Paints; *CeramDecor* **enamel satin-finish acrylic paints** from Delta Paints. Silverware caddy: *Crimson, Buttercream, Poetry Green, Red Orange,* and *Harvest Gold FolkArt Colors* **acrylic paint** from Plaid Enterprises; *Hopscotch* **stencil** from The Stencil Studio. Tool caddy: **Flatware caddy** from The Valley Forge Collection. Stools: **Unpainted stools** from Mastercraft; *Sterling Green, Poppy Red,* and *Mystic Green FolkArt Colors* **acrylic paint** from Plaid Enterprises: *Royal Coat* **decoupage medium** from Plaid Enterprises; *Green Grocer in teal* **wallcovering** (vegetable images) from Motif Designs.

---

*Any product not listed may be one-of-a kind or an antique. All the materials listed above are available at retail stores nationwide. Manufacturers' phone numbers are listed on page 128.

Directory

Artifacts, Inc.
(903) 729-4178

DCC
(316) 685-6265

Delta Paints
(800) 423-4135

Eisenhart Wallcovering
(800) 931-WALL

Hollywood Lights
(715) 834-8707

Home Decorator's
Collection
(800) 245-2217

Kiti
(div. of Woodstock
Wire Works)
(815) 338-7970

Krylon
(800) 4-KRYLON

Mastercraft
(717) 586-1811

Mill Store Products
(508) 993-1667

Motif Designs
(914) 633-1170

Plaid Enterprises, Inc.
(770) 923-8200

Provo Craft
(div. of Robert's)
(801) 373-1484

Rubber Stampede
(510) 420-6800

The Stencil Studio
(908) 236-7441

Thibaut
Wallcovering & Fabric
(973) 643-1118

The Valley Forge
Collection
(610) 277-5927

Victorian Papers
(800) 800-6647

Walnut Hollow
(800) 950-5101

Waverly
(800) 423-5881

Wood To Paint
(800) 441-9870

York Wallcovering
(800) 375-YORK

Index

Portfolio

The following pages contain extra stencil designs that you can enlarge or reduce on a photocopier for any project. They are followed by wallpaper samples that you can use for decoupage. Many of them are the same ones used in the book, but there are additional motifs, as well. If you need more than a sample, note the manufacturer and the name of the wallpaper, which is on the back of the pattern. You should be able to order any of them through a local retailer, or contact the manufacturer directly using the Directory on page 128.

WREATH

STRAWBERRY

LEAVES

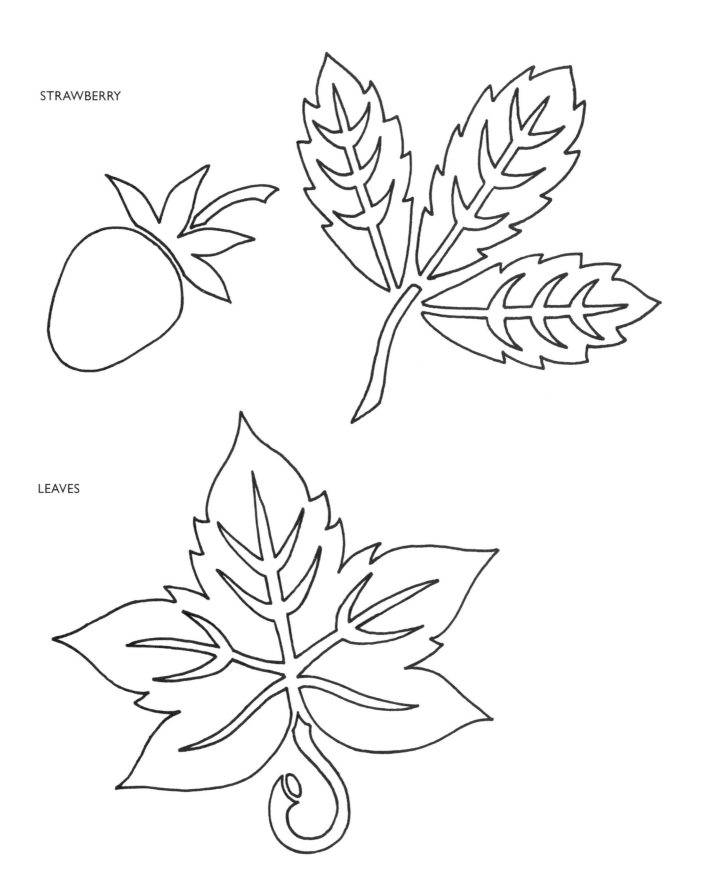

BOW

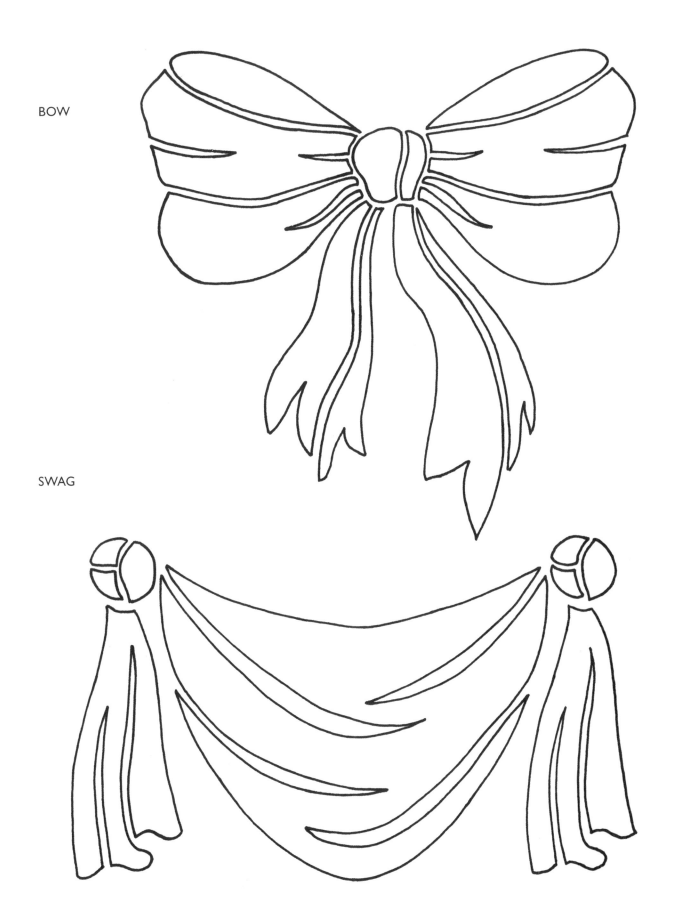

SWAG

ROPE AND TASSEL

GREEK KEY

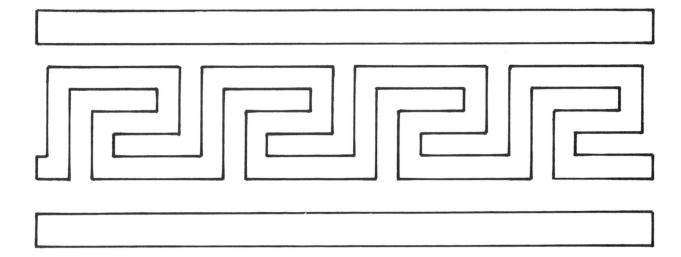

EGG-AND-DART MOLDING

PAISLEY

FISH

ANCHOR

SAILBOAT

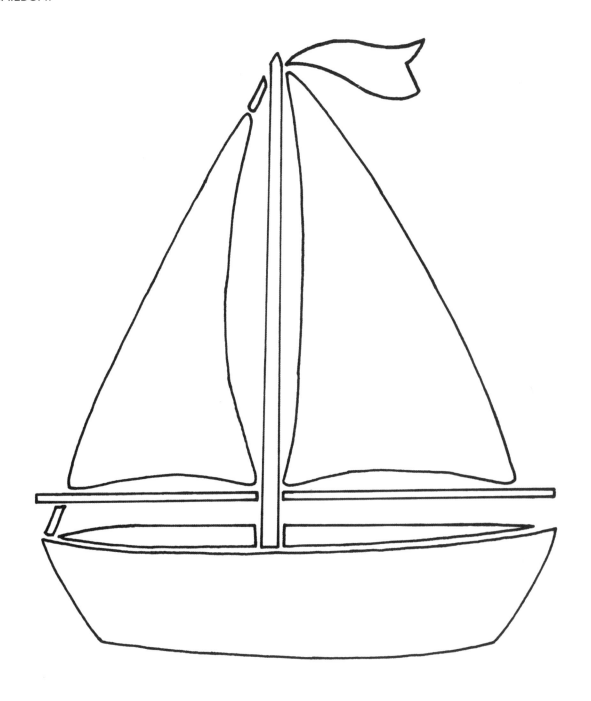

CACTUS

LIZARD

HEART

SCROLL

SHELL

BALLET SLIPPERS

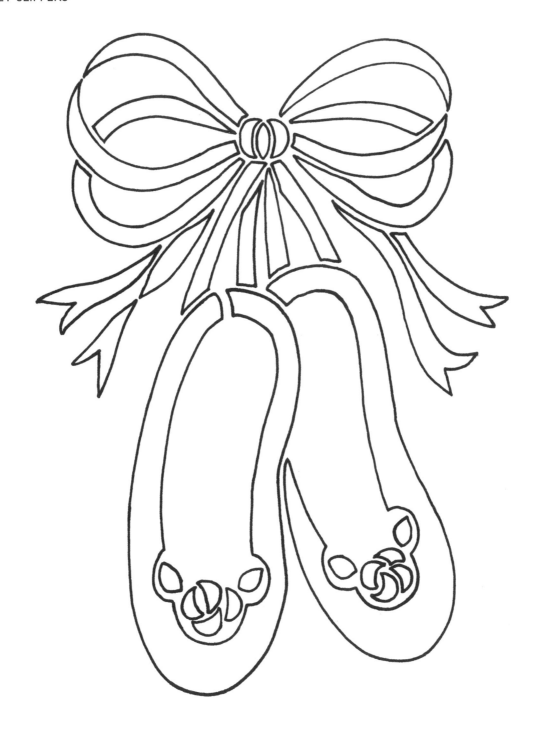

LETTERS AND NUMBERS

ABCDEFG
HIJKLMN
OPQRSTU
VWXYZ

12345
67890

Mary Rosie

from the
Vintage Rosie Collection

Design ©Motif Designs

Green Grocer

Design ©Motif Designs

Birdhouses

from the
Bluebird Hill Collection

Design ©York

Shangrila

from the
Treillage Collection

Design © Thibaut

#AD00401

from the
Victoria and Albert
Collection (volume 5)

Design ©Eisenhart

Palm Court

from the
Grand Pavilion Collection

Design © Thibaut

Puppy Love

Design ©Motif Designs

Chartier

from the
Grand Pavilion Collection

Design ©Thibaut

#HO09942

from the
Home and Office
Collection

Design ©Eisenhart

L'Arque de Paloma

Design ©Motif Designs

Apples

from the
Country Road Collection

Bombay

from the
Treillage Collection

Design ©Thibaut

#HO09921

from the
Home and Office
Collection

Design ©Eisenhart

#HO019975

from the
Home and Office
Collection

Design ©Eisenhart

Topiary

from the
Front Porch Collection

Design © Thibaut

Roosters

from the
Art Gallery Collection

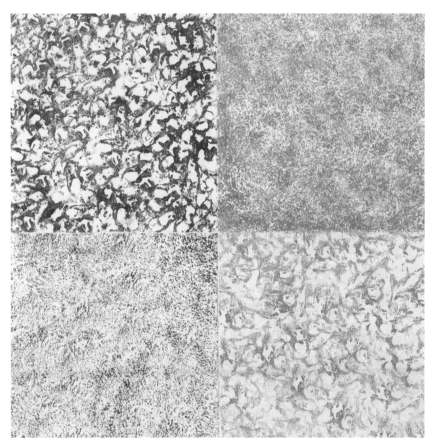

The method for sponging blocks is described on page 52.